SEA

SAMAR

MASBATE

Visayan Sea

Sea

Tacloban

LEYTE

CEBU

Toledo

Cebu Mactan I.

BOHOL

Tagbilaran

Bacolod

Ph.Camiaon

NEGROS

Iloilo

Sipalay

PANAY

Dumaguete

Mindanao Sea

Caga

Mang

M

Cota

Moro Gulf

Basilan I.

Zamboanga

CALAMIAN IS.

CUYO IS.

SULU ARCHIPELAGO

Jolo I.

Tawitawi I.

SULU     SEA

50     100     150     200

Approximate Miles

0

PALAWAN

Dorothy deFontaine 62

D1201245

# THE PHILIPPINES

*A Young Republic
on the Move*

# The Asia Library

---

THAILAND: An Introduction to Modern Siam
by NOEL F. BUSCH

CEYLON: An Introduction to the "Resplendent Land"
by ARGUS JOHN TRESIDDER

INDONESIA: A Profile
by JEANNE S. MINTZ

THE PHILIPPINES: A Young Republic on the Move
by ALBERT RAVENHOLT

The Asia Library is published in cooperation with The Asia Society, New York. Additional volumes in preparation.

# THE PHILIPPINES

## A Young Republic on the Move

ALBERT RAVENHOLT

Drawings by Manuel Rey Isip
Map by Dorothy deFontaine

D. VAN NOSTRAND COMPANY, INC.

Princeton, New Jersey

Toronto · London · New York

D. VAN NOSTRAND COMPANY, INC.
120 Alexander St., Princeton, New Jersey (*Principal office*)
24 West 40 St., New York 18, New York

D. VAN NOSTRAND COMPANY, LTD.
358, Kensington High Street, London, W.14, England

D. VAN NOSTRAND COMPANY (Canada), LTD.
25 Hollinger Road, Toronto 16, Canada

PRINTED IN THE UNITED STATES OF AMERICA
BY LANCASTER PRESS, INC., LANCASTER, PA.

# Contents

# Introduction

Enjoying, understanding, and creatively working with another people is possible only as we appreciate the perspective from which they view both the little matters of daily life and the affairs of the world. It is our purpose to encourage such an awareness of the Filipinos. We will picture their experience and environment, sketch their heritage and show what use they have made of it, and seek to discover their hopes for the future.

The Philippines is a tropical Island Republic of 28,000,000 citizens, a land of infinite variety and substantial promise that is fast becoming a modern nation. Next door lie the teeming lands of East and South Asia, their emerging new nations plagued by economic and political instability. The Philippines occupies a crucial position in this turbulent area, representing as it does the fullest development of the democratic idea on the western rim of the Pacific. While her neighbors are struggling with seemingly insurmountable problems that cripple healthy progress and inhibit individual freedom, the Philippines, some sixteen years after the achievement of full independence, has evolved a pattern of self-government that is relatively stable, that is responsive to the need for change and yet at the same time safeguards human rights. How is it that the Filipinos have afforded themselves this advantage? Does their experience relate to the problems of their neighbors? And are the Filipinos able to inspire an appreciation of their methods in fellow Asians, whose pride and new-found independence make this a delicate process at best?

Historical development and geographical location have combined to make the Philippine experience unique. During the three centuries of her rule in these Islands, Spain practiced the "most intensive Christian missionary effort in the Orient." As a consequence the Philippines today is the only predominantly Christian nation in Asia. Americans raised the Stars and Stripes over the Archipelago at the turn of the century and lent themselves to a different type of missionary enterprise. With rare energy, determination, and occasionally an overabundant faith in the rightness of their cause, they sought to build democratic institutions through public education, representative political instruments and the concept of freedom which afforded at least the promise of opportunity for all.

Filipinos have digested nearly all importations and withal usually retained their sense of personal dignity. Manila's city council occasionally does rename its streets. But generally the Philippines has been spared that curse of the new nationalisms that seeks to expunge everything the white man has brought, except his gadgets. Yet, all that has been borrowed from abroad is essentially an overlay upon indigenous institutions. Attitudes and customs that were established long before Ferdinand Magellan found his way to the Islands in 1521 still continue in evidence. So far the unique role of the family as the primary concern of the Filipino has not been erased, even in the face of industrialization, with its emphasis upon individual mobility and specialized skills. One of the riddles of the future is whether this extended familial system now can adapt itself to foster the performance that a more modern economy and state exact.

Geographically the Philippines as part of the Malayan world is situated in one of the three great areas of tropical potential (the other two are in Africa and Latin America). While most temperate lands are being exploited today within the limits of present economic technology, the development of scientific methods for the tropics is only in its infancy, and man's frontiers for feeding his burgeoning numbers lie chiefly in the moist tropics. Here in the latitude "where winter never comes" are some of the greatest of unused resources in land, minerals, fisheries, forests and power. So far the countries of Southeast Asia have progressed farther than most other regions of the moist tropics.

With the elimination of colonial rule a question arises: What is the administrative and technical potential of people never habitually compelled to discipline themselves in preparation for winter and unfamiliar with the competition for survival imposed where population presses relentlessly upon the available land? The Philippines—among the most advanced of these societies—offers both sobering and encouraging examples of what can be accomplished under their own management.

Despite the manifold problems they face in building a new nation amidst the ruins that World War II left them, Filipinos have not lost the capacity to enjoy the daily experience of living. The more intense, faster-paced societies of the West may have something to learn from a people still closer to the rhythm of nature. While politics in the Islands is an immensely consequential matter, for example, it also is a national sport. And individual concern for getting ahead in a career or business has not yet overruled attention to helping one's relatives and friends. The national delight in music and the dance, the repartee of village discussions and concern with cockfighting all demonstrate an inclination not to let mundane affairs become too serious. It is this optimistic temperament that fortifies Filipinos in adversity and helps lend the future an optimistic note amidst the uncertainties of Asia's new and cataclysmic awakening.

# 1. The Islands and the People

The environment in which Filipinos are evolving their distinctive way of life is possibly as varied as that of any people on earth. This conditions both the national temperament and prospects for the Republic. Their insular landscape has meant that Filipinos had to overcome major hurdles to build a sense of national identity—and the process is not yet complete; inhabitants of isolated islands like the windswept Batanes group north of Luzon feel themselves only remotely linked to the twentieth century mentality that dominates the thinking of citizens in Greater Manila.

Physical remoteness also poses special problems in speeding economic progress. Each Island is compelled to develop its own public services. The Republic cannot be spanned by a single electric power grid nor can commercial distribution systems readily supply the needs of such isolated Filipinos as the residents of the Cuyo Group in the Sulu Sea. Delivering the mail on time and undamaged becomes a real challenge to the ingenuity of the postal service. It is also this fragmented character of the Archipelago, with large and small islands guarding enclosed seas, that creates a particular beauty, as coconut palms lean over the coral formations and white sand beaches and are silhouetted against the lush green slopes farther inland.

The sovereignty of the Republic includes some 7,100 islands; the total figure actually changes as new islands are "born" through volcanic action occasionally pushing up another isle, that later may be washed away by the Pacific. These islands extend for 1,200 miles from 5 degrees north of the equator just east of British Borneo to within sight of the rocks that mark Formosa's southern outposts. They help shield the South China Sea and its necklace of new tropical nations from the Pacific storms, including both the northeast monsoons and the destructive typhoons that originate near Guam. These sweep westward to spend part of their fury over Luzon and the Visayas or are deflected north toward Formosa, Okinawa and the China mainland. Warm waters gathered from these shallow seas help form the Japan Current, the Kuroshio, that moderates the climate along its course past the Ryukyus and the Aleutians to the coast of British Columbia and the States of Washington and Oregon.

In total land area the Philippines is approximately equal to Great Britain or the New England states and New York combined. But the actual land surface of 115,600 square miles comprises only about one-sixth of the national domain; the remainder is composed of surrounding waters over which the Republic claims jurisdiction and such near-land-locked bodies of water as the Mindanao Sea, the Sibuyan Sea, the fabled Sulu Sea and numerous straits. Although an exact measurement has never been made, the total coastline of all the Islands combined may exceed that of the United States. Luzon and Mindanao forming the northern and southern anchors of the Archipelago contain roughly two-thirds of the total land and are almost "continental" in character. They hold substantial plains like those of Central Luzon, the northeastern Cagayan Valley and, in the far south, the Agusan basin and the wide rolling landscape of Cotabato that are girded by mountains and drained by large rivers. Of major importance to Filipinos are nine other islands: Cebu, Negros, Bohol, Panay, Leyte and Samar which almost join, Masbate, Mindoro, and Palawan. They range in size from 1,250 to 5,000 square miles, as

3

contrasted to another 455 islands that each hold from 1 to 500 square miles. The remaining more than 6,500 islands are of little economic consequence and over 4,000 of them have been given no names on published maps, although Filipinos who live on or near these isles use local terms to describe each, sometimes after an incident related to the site or a curious formation that has aroused popular interest.

Scientists are still reconstructing the history of the geological ages when the Philippines was formed. Although the Philippines is perched along the rim of the Western Pacific trench that leads south from near Japan past Formosa to the deepest known spot on earth off eastern Mindanao—the ocean bottom here is more than six miles beneath the surface—the Islands do not appear to be a true extension of the Asiatic shelf. Rather, they have been cast up, broken apart and worn down to be lifted again above the Pacific by the mighty tectonic movements in the earth's crust that have characterized this region. The larger islands were shoved up from the ocean floor as the crests of anticlinal folds and as upthrust blocks caused by faulting; in Northern Luzon there are ancient coral formations that now rest more than a mile above sea level. With the exception of the Sulu Sea which in places is three and one-half miles deep, the water between these islands generally is shallow. Here the numerous coral formations have built up to form many of the small

4

isles that are strung like glittering pearls through the central and southern regions of the Archipelago.

To this largely tectonic process has been added intense volcanic activity; most of these volcanos have died down and become eroded but some forty still are more or less active. One chain of volcanos leads north from Borneo through Palawan and Mindoro to Western and Northern Luzon. Another such volcanic line evidently extended from Borneo through the Sulu Archipelago and Western Mindanao into Negros where majestic Mount Canlaon stands as a still active sentinel, having disgorged the debris that formed the rich coastal plains of this sugar growing region. Two other chains of volcanos extended north and south through Central and Eastern Mindanao. One of these is marked today by the enormous crater that holds Lake Lanao some 2,000 feet above sea level and the adjacent Mount Ragang to the south where a cluster of volcanic cones rises to roughly 10,000 feet in occasionally furious activity. The other chain begins with 10,000-foot Mount Apo near Davao, includes the volcano that now periodically rains destruction on Camiguin Island and extends through Leyte and Samar up the Bicol Peninsula into the Sierra Madre Range and the "cradle of volcanos" southeast of Manila Bay. Both to the geologist and to the devotee of beauty in nature this chain offers spectacular attractions. At the very southern tip of Luzon stands

5,115-foot Mount Bulusan, which is still active, over-
looking the San Bernardino Strait that opens onto
the stormy Pacific. Near Legaspi is steaming Mount
Mayon which rises 7,960 feet to form the most per-
fect volcanic cone in the world. Mount Banahao within
sight of Laguna de Bay is nearly as high and is flanked
by its nearby smaller neighbor, Mount Makiling. Farther to the west is the favorite tourist attraction of
the huge Taal volcanic crater, now holding a lake with
its own smaller and still active volcano inside; much
of Greater Manila rests upon ashes thrown up long
ago by this volcano to form the adobe stone quarried
for building and numerous other purposes.

Like most of the lands that ring the Pacific, the
Philippines is subject to frequent and sometimes severe earthquakes. This violent movement in the earth's
crust over eons of time has opened numerous fault
lines; some can be seen, such as one huge crack in the
floor of Ragay Gulf off Southern Luzon. It is these
fault lines that have facilitated extrusion of the minerals including gold, copper, lead, zinc, chromite and
others still being explored. But the process of geologic
formation may have so fractured the Islands as to
minimize the prospects of major petroleum deposits.
The origin and dating of the land bridges that during
several geologic periods linked the Philippines to present day Borneo, Sumatra and the Asian mainland still
are in dispute. But it is generally agreed that the

6

Islands lie at the northern terminus of the Wallace Line, that remarkable demarcation extending from the Lombok Strait east of Bali north through the Makassar Strait into the Philippines. The co-discoverer of the "theory of natural selection," Alfred Russell Wallace, found that this line tended to divide the forms of life associated with the Asian mainland from those that had originated in and around Australia. As the "bridge" over which these forms of flora and fauna were able to intermingle, the Philippines evolved an extraordinary variety of species and became a botanical wonderland.

A traveler through the Islands is impressed with the variety of climates at differing elevations and the great contrasts in types of landscape encountered. This traces in part to the weather; a single island may have two or three distinct rainfall patterns. Northwestern and Central Luzon have a definite dry season extending approximately through the first half of the year, while the rains brought by the northeast monsoons are captured by the mountain slopes facing the Pacific. This pattern is almost equally characteristic of the western portions of Mindoro, Panay, Negros and Palawan. Later, the start of the southwest monsoon brings intense precipitation to these areas, while the eastern regions of the Bicol Peninsula, Samar, Leyte and Mindanao experience their driest months. A central belt extending from Southern Mindanao through

the Visayas to the Cagayan Valley has a more mod-
erated rainfall with local variations influenced by to-
pography. In most settled communities the annual
rainfall ranges from 43 inches to about 170 inches.
Particularly when a typhoon spills its enormous load
of moisture, a concentrated downpour may flood rivers,
washing out bridges and dikes; the summer capital of
Baguio once experienced a rainfall of 133 inches in a
single month.

The vegetation encouraged by this abundance of
moisture, by the considerable areas of fertile, volcani-
cally deposited soils often overlaying limestone, and
by the differences in temperature has been affected also
by man's relentless determination to subdue the jungle.
From the cool, pine-clad mountain crests of Northern
Luzon to the mangrove swamps along the Moro Gulf,
forest can be found cloaking nearly one-half of the
land surface. At some of the higher elevations where
rainfall is intense and continues throughout most of
the year there are fog-shrouded, moss-laden growths
almost impenetrable to man. In the forests on the
lower slopes dipterocarps usually form the top story
of the jungle. The commercial stands of timber include 65 species and cover some 23,000,000 acres that
provide the basis for a growing export industry sup-
plying Philippine Mahogany to much of the world. Another 9,500,000 acres are classed as noncommercial
forest. In addition to stands of timber the forests

support a luxuriant growth of numerous shade-loving plants and vines including rattan, sometimes 200 yards long, that finds favor with furniture makers. On the lower slopes are also found palms of several dozen kinds, the distinctive fig tree, numerous species of graceful bamboo, wild cinnamon and hundreds of plants for which medical uses have been discovered, to mention only a few. In all approximately 15,000 flowering plants have been identified and nearly 1,000 native orchids. Some 13,500,000 acres are occupied by the tall, tough cogon grass and brush that often have grown up after the destructive *caingin* farming whereby the forest is burned to afford fertility for two or three crops before the migratory cultivators move on to another site. Of the remaining 28,000,000 acres nearly 2,000,000 are covered by swamps, some of which have been converted into fish ponds and salt beds. It is estimated that some 16,500,000 acres of this area now is cultivated and that introduction of suitable farming methods might permit doubling this arable area.

The fauna of the Philippine Archipelago is almost as varied as its flora, although most of the larger wild animals found on mainland Southeast Asia, including the tiger, seladang, elephant and rhinoceros, no longer inhabit the Islands. Largest among the wild life on land today is the *tamarao*, characteristic particularly of Mindoro, a wild buffalo, not much different from the domesticated *carabao*. In the jungle the wild pig abounds, to the delight of the sportsman and distress of the farmer whose crops it roots out. In less inhabited regions deer are plentiful, including the mouse deer of Palawan that is reputed to be the smallest in the world. Bird life is extraordinarily abundant and many have brilliant plumage; some 750 species have been identified, including the famed monkey-eating eagle. Some remote regions are favored by huge bats living in caves where they deposit their guano that farmers prize for fertilizer. They emerge at night to feed on jungle fruits in such numbers that they blanket the sky. Monkeys are found throughout the Islands and the Philippines has supplied many chartered plane-loads for research laboratories in the West; while some naturalists deplore the trapping of these agile inhabitants of the jungle, farmers on the frontier are glad to be rid of those that become pests and dig out newly planted coconut trees. Rodents and particularly rats inhabiting the swamps often are a curse on new settlers; they nest in the crowns of coconut trees and destroy the flowers, climb cacao trees to eat the pods and, particularly in Cotabato, move in enormous flocks that destroy a corn field in a single night despite efforts to fight them off with fire and ditches. Elegant butterflies and insects are found in this region in possibly greater profusion than anywhere else in the world, but much research remains to be done in classifying them.

Crocodiles once were numerous in Philippine swamps and streams. But the growing world demand for their skins has led to intensive hunting. Their smaller reptilian relatives are represented in abundance, including the tiny lizards that nest in Filipino homes and delight in hunting mosquitos on the walls and ceiling. Snakes likewise are numerous and include pythons, several types of cobras and other poisonous members of their family such as sea serpents. The green turtle, or *Chelonia mydas,* favors the Sulu Sea and annually millions of its eggs are gathered from islands in this region. Philippine waters a century ago were frequented by whaling ships, but today most of the whales have moved to other feeding grounds. The sea cow or *dugong*—a tropical mammal of the ocean whose body measures up to 12 feet in length—still abounds, as do several kinds of sharks. Some 2,400 species of fish inhabit the waters of the Archipelago, including tuna, the locally prized *lapu lapu* and many others of commercial value, and the smallest fish in the world, the *Pondoka pygmaea.* Conchologists find the reefs and shallow waters among the Islands a uniquely productive area that so far has yielded about 10,000 different species of shell life. These include some of lovely color and form that protect themselves with poisonous stings, the giant clams or *tridacna* that measure up to four feet in length and oysters that in some waters grow to a diameter of more than ten inches.

In keeping with their maritime traditions the Filipinos who inhabit this landscape are concentrated primarily near the seashore and in selected interior settings where man has mastered nature, pushing back the jungle. Burgeoning population within recent decades is now bringing the first acute pressure of people against available resources in some of these areas. The old church records from the Spanish period state that in the year 1800 there were 1,561,251 persons in the Islands; this figure did not include the Moros and other non-Christian groups. By 1845 the Christian population was recorded as having increased to 3,488,258. The U. S. authorities took their first official census in 1902, counting 6,987,686 Christianized Filipinos and 647,740 "wild people" or a total population of 7,635,426. By 1918 the Philippine population numbered 10,314,310, reflecting an annual increase of about 2.3 percent. The census published in 1939 indicated by then the population had grown to 16,000,303. Filipinos, numbering approximately 28,000,000 in 1961, are increasing their population by some 900,000 or 3.2 percent annually. And indications are that with a declining mortality, particularly among infants, the net rate of increase may be further accelerated before the close of this century.

So far this "population explosion" has been less evident among the non-Christians composing the colorful minorities scattered throughout the Islands; in their communities there has been scant attention to modern health and technology. Nearly one out of every ten Filipinos belongs to one of these ethnic groups that largely have retained their former customs and religious practices. While they share least in the national political process and the advantages it disposes, these minorities also constitute a major challenge to the conscience of the Republic, much as do the Indians in the American West. For them the problem arises of how they can participate in the benefits that twentieth century knowledge affords for a better life and yet be permitted to retain their indigenous values and treasured institutions.

The minority peoples about whom we possess the most detailed understanding are the mountain peoples of Northern Luzon—sometimes they are referred to as Igorots, but actually they form distinct tribes of Ifugaos, Bontocs, Benguets, Kalingas and Apayaos and lesser known groups whose total numbers exceed some 300,000. It is they, and particularly the most numerous Ifugaos, who have become noted for their engineering skill in building the rice terraces that have stood for centuries as gigantic man-made steps permitting the intensive cultivation of precipitous mountain slopes. This achievement represents more than skillful use of brawn and simple tools to move rock and earth. It is the expression of a highly developed and cohesive society with its own systems of law, water rights, land ownership, inheritance and authority, worked out long ago. These highland people especially have attracted the attention of the outside world with their practice of head-taking, which actually is a highly ritualized form of blood feud that may lead to intervillage warfare; it is still practiced occasionally when the Philippine Constabulary is not much in evidence. Colorful, handwoven G-strings are worn by the men and the women clothe themselves in brilliant skirts. Razor-sharp spears carried both for defense and as symbols of status are prized by the older men, particularly among the nobles forming the elite of the community. But many of the younger men and women are beginning to seek opportunity outside and are bringing home a taste for modern gadgets, food and dress. And as the native rice wine that is consumed on ceremonial and festive occasions gives way to a liking for coffee and soft drinks, such former customs as the capacity to recite one's genealogy over the past sixteen generations tend to be ignored.

Far more of a problem to the Philippine authorities are the Ilongots and their less numerous aboriginal neighbors who live in the mountains farther east and south, particularly in the provinces of Nueva Viscaya, Isabela, Nueva Ecija and Quezon. They are a secretive, nomadic people who depend upon hunting and a primitive agriculture. Their periodic raids into the Christian lowlands in search of victims whose heads they can bring home to their mountain villages as evidence of male prowess make them a continuing terror to their more settled neighbors who do not prize the warlike professions. Farther south and west across the Central Luzon Plain in the Zambales Mountains live the Aetas. They are a furtive, suspicious and less highly organized minority which has suffered from repeated encroachment of Christians upon their lands. Like the Mangyans of Mindoro, the Ibanags of the Bicol Peninsula, the Negritos of Negros and such Eastern Mindanao tribes as the Manobos, Bukidnons and Bagobos, they practice an upland agriculture, burning forest patches for new fields. They supplement their livelihood with game and fruit from the jungle. The diversity of these and other smaller tribes, their scattered settlements and lack of knowledge about the modern world, make their existence increasingly marginal. Despite creation of a National Integration Commission intended to bring these peoples modern education and health services, they have been unable to secure the political representation that more adequate attention to their needs and traditional rights would require.

By contrast the largest minority in the Islands, the Muslim Moros, are in the process of mobilizing their numbers to insure a voice in national affairs. Included among these are the fierce Maranaws who dominate the Lanao Plateau, Maguindanaos and their kin in Cotabato, the Tao Suug of the Sulu Archipelago, their neighbors, the Samals or Sea Moros and the Badjaos, otherwise known as sea gypsies, who spend their lives on houseboats, fishing, hunting for turtle eggs and trading. During the centuries when they fought off Spanish efforts to subdue and Christianize them, these Moros developed the cult of the warrior. Although the young Maranao may have replaced his curve-bladed *kris* with a modern pistol, he still learns to sing the *darangan* or ancient ballad and memorizes the Koran in Arabic. Smuggling and piracy in the waters around Sulu and cattle rustling on Mindanao are considered semi-legitimate professions by many young Moros, much to the distress of Philippine officials. Although their communities still are dominated by hierarchies of *datus*—or chieftains—and sultans whose power is reinforced by religion and kinship ties, this pattern of authority is being modified through elective government. A datu may deliver all the votes of his villages to one set of party candidates and maintain a padded roster that no Christian inspector from Manila readily can check. But he justifies this on grounds of insuring attention to the needs of his people. While the past suspicion of education among Moros has meant that today few are schooled in medicine or trained as teachers, these Muslims are electing their own officials including representatives to Congress. As a consequence they are increasingly able to retain the lands they claim through hereditary right and moderate the application of the national legal system to accommodate indigenous traditions. In this new-found assurance of a voice in national affairs lies the strongest guarantee that the Moros, while maintaining their distinct cultural identity, also will view themselves as Filipinos and citizens of the Republic.

The dominant character of the Philippine nation is determined by the Christians, who constitute approximately 90 percent of the populace. However, within this majority there are major ethnic divisions. Each shares a distinct heritage and mother tongue which encourages its members to act together and has fostered common cultural traits. The barriers represented by these ethnographic distinctions are diminishing, due to increasing physical mobility, the move toward urbanization and intermarriage and the development of national tastes and attitudes as a result of mass communications media. Yet, the pattern of settlement on the new frontiers and the traits that guide Filipinos in their political allegiances as in their

17

choice of careers can partly be distinguished through a consideration of these origins.

Traditionally, the most industrious, venturesome and ambitious among the inhabitants of the Archipelago are the Ilocanos whose homeland is on the narrow, dry and comparatively infertile coast of Northwestern Luzon. Here is found the most dense concentration of rural population; La Union Province holds some 1,400 residents per square mile. Composing about 12 percent of the Filipino people, the Ilocanos are motivated by competition for land at home, a strong admixture of Chinese blood and long contact with the sea to become pioneers. It is they who often have crossed over the mountains to the east and settled in still virgin regions of the great Cagayan River Valley. They are prominent among the new settlers sailing south to open the plains and highlands of Mindanao and provided most of the immigrants who have found employment and homes in Hawaii and on the west coast of the United States. On Luzon Ilocanos also have moved south to settle among the original inhabitants of Pangasinan and Zambales, who once composed distinct linguistic minorities, and have opened some of the new communities in Nueva Ecija as well.

The center of the productive rice-growing plain in the heart of Luzon is the homeland of the Pampangeños who comprise nearly 3½ percent of the populalation. Traditionally, they are farmers and possibly the most skilled in the Philippines. Among other Filipinos they have acquired the reputation for being sharp businessmen and sometimes shrewd moneylenders. Their neighbors to the south are the Tagalogs who inhabit the environs of Greater Manila and lands to the east. Approximately one out of every five Filipinos is a Tagalog. It is they more than any other ethnic group who have given their stamp to the national prototype. A preponderance of the independence leaders in late Spanish times, like many writers, poets and doctors, were Tagalogs. This was likewise true of some of the more vigorous, modern political leaders including Commonwealth President Manuel Quezon. Such early leadership of intellectual and political life, their numerical prominence in the civil service and Manila's dominant cultural role made Tagalog the favorite of vernacular movies and the basis for the national language now being created. Although other Filipinos may accuse Tagalogs of a proclivity for leaving the capital chiefly as bureaucrats assigned to the provinces, they are leaders among the entrepreneurs and engineers building the new industries. While their speech includes many Spanish words, the Caviteños to the South also are Tagalogs, like their neighbors the Batangeños. Both are noted for their fiery temper and scorn for authority; the popular image holds that natives of Cavite are more inclined to express this

19

by leading away someone else's *carabao* while people from Batangas vent their feelings over political issues.

The narrow southern peninsula of Luzon is the domain of the Bicolanos, a people made hardy by centuries of braving the Pacific typhoons and accustomed to living off the sea. Credited in folklore with a "passive, romantic soul," this distinct ethnic group composes about 8 percent of the total population. They share many traits with the Samareños of the Eastern Visayas who are almost equally numerous. In the Central Visayas live the Cebuanos, the largest single linguistic group, among whom is numbered one out of every four Filipinos. Conditioned by population pressure and limited natural resources on Bohol, Cebu, and adjacent areas, they have aggressively developed skills and sought opportunity in maritime professions and on the Mindanao frontier. Western Negros, Panay and some of the neighboring smaller islands where Hiligaynon-speaking Filipino Christians predominate afford many fertile farming opportunities, encouraging stable communities long linked by extensive kinship patterns. Wealth generated here in modern times made its leading families noted as conspicuous consumers and prominent financiers of politics and new commercial enterprises.

Cities grew up in each of these population centers during the Spanish era, and their commercial role was vastly enhanced with the expansion of trade following establishment of the U. S. administration. Iloilo, traditionally the entrepôt for sugar exports and Panay's cattle trade, now is giving way to the newer and more aggressive city of Bacolod, that also is the capital of Negros Occidental. Dumaguete retains its charm as a quiet provincial capital and university town spread between the coconut-tree clad slopes behind and its bund affording a delightful promenade along the waterfront. The commercial hub of the central and southern Philippines and second most important port of the Islands is Cebu, which retains its massive monuments to early Spanish settlement here despite wartime fires that ravaged much of the city and led to extensive rebuilding. Half a dozen cities are growing as the wealth of Mindanao is opened for exploitation. Iligan, below the Maria Cristina Falls, promises to become the new industrial center of the South. Cagayan de Oro, Butuan, Cotabato, and particularly Davao, all are boom towns, complete with their growing pains and subdivisions. While it is one of the best managed and most delightful among metropolitan communities in the Islands, Zamboanga continues to reflect its older origins and the adventurous instincts of its Moro neighbors, whose sleek sailing craft crowd its port alongside foreign merchant vessels loading copra and other cargo from the hinterland. Older cities of the Eastern Visayas such as Tagbilaran on Bohol and Tacloban on Leyte, which felt the full force of the American liberation campaigns in 1944, have been less favored by post-independence progress. Like Legaspi, which is the chief port for the Bicol Peninsula, they have continued in the provincial way of life with its leisurely pace of business. This is equally true of the old Ilocos towns of Laoag and Vigan with their massive Spanish-period cathedrals and memories of a revolutionary past.

Industry's dramatic impact and twentieth century modernization are remaking urban life most impatiently around the heart of Luzon. Both Batangas, and Mariveles on Bataan, today hold major oil refineries processing imported crude to supply the burgeoning Philippine market for petroleum products. Olongapo, which lies next to the U. S. Naval base at Subic, and Angeles, adjacent to the U. S. Clark Air Base-Fort Stotsenburg Reservation in Central Luzon, are a garish commercial reflection of expanded American military expenditures. All through this region, from San Fernando above Lingayen Gulf past Dagupan and Tarlac south to Cavite and the college town of Los Baños on the southern shores of Laguna de Bay, the traditional nipa palm-thatched homes are giving way to modern concrete structures. Gasoline filling stations are appearing on street corners and the tempo of human activity is being accelerated. Sitting apart and a mile above it all on the pine-clad mountain ridges to the north is the summer capital of Baguio. Levelled by

the war but now a mecca of Filipino business, professional and political leaders seeking leisure, Baguio is
also experiencing growing pains, as elaborate new
bungalows line the hillsides around the golf courses
and the presidential retreat at Mansion House.

The pace and pattern for this new way of Filipino
urbanized and industrialized living are being set by
Greater Manila which holds more than 2,500,000
residents—nearly one-tenth of the national population.
It is here that most important careers and decisions
are made. Annually tens of thousands of young Filipinos flock in searching for higher education and opportunity. Actually, Greater Manila is a complex of
cities, each more or less autonomous. The core of this
metropolis is Manila proper, which long ago outgrew
the confines of the original Spanish walled city of
Intramuros and the commercial districts along the
Pasig River. South along the Bay stretch Pasay and
Parañaque. Further inland lies Makati, which holds
some of the plushiest suburbs in Asia, and the cities
of Mandaluyong and San Juan del Monte. Geographically, the largest of all is Quezon City, reaching out
toward the foothills of the Sierra Madre; it is the
official national capital, although Congress and most
government bureaus remain at their former locations
in downtown Manila and the presidential residence
continues to be Malacañang Palace. North along the

Bay the newly chartered city of Caloocan extends toward the fish ponds of Malabon and Navotas.

This metropolitan complex is experiencing a major and visible metamorphosis. Clusters of miserable squatter shacks, a heritage of war, increasingly are overshadowed by the adventurous architecture of glass-cased office buildings and multi-storied apartments. Particularly in the district of Ermita behind Dewey Boulevard, European restaurants and ultramodern shop fronts are spreading out behind the air-conditioned hotels that face the Bay. A scattered profusion of small machine shops, garages for building the "jeepneys" that have become the "poor man's taxi," sawmills and warehouses all give evidence of the new concern with manufacturing. The steel outlines of dozens of new factories that symbolize the conversion of Greater Manila into an industrial giant are silhouetted along the skyline adjoining the Pasig River and extending out into the Marikina Valley. Manila also remains the chief port for inter-island and international trade. The magnificent trees that were the pride of Manila's streets were broken by artillery fire and tanks during the war and have yet to be fully replaced. But the city is beginning to recapture some of its former grace. A traveler from Tokyo or New York landing at the International Airport and motoring into the heart of Manila or debarking from a liner in the South Harbor would feel

24

comparatively at home among the noisy traffic jams, neon-lit signs, plush movie theaters, night clubs and supermarkets, although on the horizon some forty miles to the east he could see the virtually unexplored jungles of the cordillera facing the Pacific.

Greater Manila also is home to most of the alien minorities that directly or in partnership with Filipinos fulfill a vital role in the life of the Republic. Chief among these are the Chinese, numbering roughly half a million in the Islands. Nearly every community of consequence in the provinces has its one or several Chinese merchants. They dominate the retail trade, provide a vital source of rural credit and increasingly share in opening new industries; some also are philanthropists, since the Chinese long ago discovered that they prosper best in a healthy town. But it is in the national metropolis that their cultural institutions best can be distinguished. Here are the streets where Chinese dealers selling automobile parts speak the Amoy dialect of their ancestral homes in Fukien Province as often as Tagalog or English. While the more prosperous families have expanded their shops into modern self-service markets and occasionally converted a hardware store into an assembly plant, the former Chinese trade associations remain strong. Chinese schools, restaurants, cemeteries and theaters all are maintained by this energetic minority that remains loyal to its cultural heritage. Like German, Italian,

Scandinavian and other ethnic colonies of the midwestern United States, Chinese in the Philippines see no dichotomy between such special institutions and allegiance to the Republic. Filipinos, however, frequently fear and resent both the Chinese economic success and past ties to a now hostile homeland. Indian and Pakistani minorities performing a similar function are so much smaller that they rarely become targets for hostility. An Indonesian minority of some 6,000 is found chiefly along the southern fringes of Mindanao, far from centers of national attention. As the commercial and political capital, Greater Manila also holds substantial communities of Spanish, British, German, Swiss and other Europeans plus Japanese and Americans. U.S. citizens in the Islands number about 25,000 and nearly an equal number, including men in uniform and their dependents, reside at the military bases. Although they maintain their special clubs and churches, the cosmopolitan character of the capital and emphasis upon western modes of life and dress make them less conspicuous than in most Asian countries.

## 2. Early History and Spanish Rule

Filipinos have begun to form a clear estimate of their own origins only within recent decades. As this sense of continuity with a more distant past grows upon the national consciousness it fosters the added confidence that most of us gain from having honored ancestors. For it is part of the price of a colonial heritage that it often tends to divorce a people from ties with their native culture in its most sophisticated forms of expression. In a country such as the Philippines, where intensive introductions of Spanish and American customs and values predominated for three and one-half centuries, foreign goals and modes of living are substituted at the apex of the society. In the process, legends, artifacts and traditions of an earlier and largely prehistoric era tend to survive only at the fringes of the dominant culture. These historical gaps are being filled in, due in large measure to research by Western scholars who were attracted to the Islands during the period of American administration. And we are now able to form an image of events during the unrecorded millennia when the Filipino way of life was born.

The Philippine Islands first were host to human inhabitants about 250,000 years ago, archeologists now believe. On the main island of Luzon they have found stone implements and other evidence of these primitive people who resembled the Java Man. Several theories have been developed to account for their origins. But most scholars believe that they wandered in from the south and west over land bridges that then joined the Malay Peninsula and Sumatra with Borneo and the Philippines. On detailed charts of the waters of the South China Sea these now submerged land masses still can be traced. Other forms of life including the rhinoceros, the stegadon and a pygmy-type elephant may have arrived by the same route; their remains have been uncovered in the northeastern Cagayan River Valley, where geologists today are searching for petroleum deposits. These large mammals, like the earliest human inhabitants, became extinct long before the beginning of the most recent glacial period, leaving only their skeletons as evidence of their existence.

A great "in-gathering" of many and varied peoples at a much later period composed the ancestors of present-day Filipinos. The first of these were pygmy Negritos arriving overland some 25,000 to 30,000 years ago. Their descendants still have dark, tightly curled hair, the adults may average below four and one-half feet in height and they now inhabit isolated mountain areas on several of the larger islands.

An ethnically very different type of people followed. Originally, most of these folk appear to have wandered down from deep in the hinterland of Asia along the major river valleys such as those of the Mekong and Yangtze. Encouraged to seek new frontiers, in part by the pressure of expanding populations behind them such as the Chinese or Han, they moved into Southeast Asia. Some 15,000 years ago or less representatives of these short Mongoloid people also arrived in the Philippines over the land bridges. They brought the first crude agriculture to the Islands, burning clearings in the forest and planting root crops and bananas to supplement the game they hunted with the blowgun and bows and arrows or caught in traps.

The sea was the highway, however, that carried most of the original settlers to the Islands and a fondness for remaining near the water is stamped upon the national consciousness. The first of these water-borne settlers are believed to have come from the north about 5,000 to 6,000 years ago, probably by way of East China and Formosa. The builders of the sturdy boats that could navigate these seas of the Western Pacific also possessed an advanced culture as a New Stone Age people. Their polished stone axes and other tools enabled them to build permanent homes with stone walls and quonset-shaped grass covered round roofs. Agricultural innovations they introduced included the planting and cultivation of upland rice and possibly other grains. A second and larger influx of immigrant seafaring people began after 2,000 B.C. Coming from the region of South China, Hainan Island, and Vietnam, they likewise settled along the numerous protected bays character-istic of the Islands and moved up the most accessible rivers.

Irrigated rice cultivation which requires advanced skills and tools and considerable social organization reached the Philippines only some 2,700 years ago. It was brought from the Southeast Asian mainland by a comparatively small migration of people who had developed the manufacture of bronze weapons and tools and also used jade ornaments. In time, growing of rice in paddy fields was adopted by earlier settlers and extended to the mountainous areas. They offered greater security and freedom from ma-laria but enormous labor was needed here for construction of paddy fields. The earliest of the famed rice terraces of Mountain Province in Northern Luzon—classed as an eighth wonder of the world—date from soon after this period; they are made possible only by a highly intricate control of water for irrigation and preservation of forest cover on the upper slopes, so necessary to controlling erosion. Along with the cultivation of irrigated rice developed the domestication of the *carabao,* or water buffalo, and the introduction of domesticated pigs and fowl, also from the Southeast Asian mainland.

The largest migration of people to the Islands occurred about 300 to 200 B.C. with the influx of the Malays who brought their iron age tools, pottery making, and weaving. Traveling in large canoes hollowed from tree trunks, they moved up the coast of Borneo and by way of the Sulu Archipelago and Palawan to settle chiefly on the Central Visayan Islands, Mindoro, and Southwestern Luzon. As each of these successive waves of immigrants arrived they either displaced the earlier inhabitants along the coast or blended with them. This pattern of settlement encouraged the great linguistic fragmentation that continues to this day; verbal differentiation resulted as newcomers arrived from such varied regions of Asia to establish their homes on an island cove or in a mountain valley and developed distinct language habits to fit their needs. The fifty-five separate ethnic

31

groups now identifiable speak some seventy mother tongues, although the eight principal native languages for which there is a limited written literature are in use by more than 80 percent of the population.

A new chapter of the Philippine saga is now being opened as archeologists bring to light a surprising wealth of sites inhabited by Filipinos during the first millennium and a half of the Christian era. It is evident that during this period, of which we have only the scantiest written records, inhabitants of the Islands did not coalesce into a powerful centralized state. Instead, Filipinos were organized into numerous largely self-contained communities, sometimes known as *barangays,* after the craft in which the Malay settlers had arrived. Such a community might include a hundred or more families linked to each other by complex kinship patterns. A *datu,* or chieftain, usually headed the *barangay* and was assisted in its management by a class of hereditary nobles. There were also freemen and a subservient class bound in status to follow the directions of its betters in war and work. Filipino communities of this period—with the exception of minorities who settled in the mountains—usually were established near the water-borne trade routes, where harbors offered shelter from storms or promontories afforded protection. Other populous centers grew up along the shores of Laguna de Bay, the large fresh water lake that feeds into Manila Bay from the east.

Lingayen Gulf on Northwestern Luzon, where Japanese and American invading forces landed during World War II, served as a point of entry to a now silted up water route south across the Central Luzon Plain. Before great eruptions of the Taal volcano buried their villages under ashes, a substantial population inhabited the present-day provinces of Batangas and Cavite, particularly abreast of the Verde Island Passage. Despite such repeated destruction raining from the skies this region was peopled again by newcomers or neighbors who moved in on the fertile soils.

For that time many of these communities were comparatively sophisticated. A larger trading center that served an important hinterland often included among its residents Chinese, Indian, and occasionally Arab, merchants. They added words to the local language, occasionally introduced elements of their religious practices, married into local families and contributed their genes to the race. These communities enjoyed substantial contact with the outside world through trade and travel. Over the comparatively calm waters that link the lands of Southeast Asia journeyed Arab, Indian, and other merchants and adventurers in their fast sailing craft. These included Sinbad the Sailor and Marco Polo, who have left accounts of their travels that are known in the West. Although the Chinese were active participants in this trade from very early times, they only became dominant in such

33

commerce after establishment of the Southern Sung Dynasty in 1127. However, Chinese porcelains from earlier periods such as the T'ang (618–906) were used as articles of commerce. And beads made in Bactria, the ancient Iranian kingdom of the Hindu Kush, a century or two before the birth of Christ found their way to the Islands together with rare artifacts from other distant lands. Recent archeological finds show evidence of substantial trade with the lands today known as Thailand, Cambodia, and Vietnam and some with the south coast of India. Filipinos paid for imported manufactures with the famed pearls of the Sulu Archipelago prized by Oriental potentates, rare woods, medicinal plants, and other products of the sea and forest. Before the Chinese developed their own domestic growing of cotton the Ilocos coast of northwestern Luzon was a major exporter; huge Chinese junks arrived annually on the monsoon winds to load and carry back their valued cargoes.

At one period only did the Philippines experience the historical tendency of the Chinese imperial colossus to dominate its smaller neighbors. During the reign of the Ming Emperor Yung Lo (1405–1435), the Chinese appointed a governor for Luzon and exacted tribute. It was then that Admiral Cheng-Ho, the Chinese eunuch and master organizer, built his great fleets of junks, sailing into Manila Bay and touching at other islands. His voyages carried him into the Indian Ocean and were part of an abortive Chinese enterprise to claim sovereignty beyond the seas. Failure of the Chinese to incorporate the Philippine Islands more permanently into the empire ruled from Peking, as they did periodically with Tonkin, Annam, and sections of Burma, was due less to resistance by the inhabitants than to political shifts among the Ming rulers. The Chinese abandoned the opportunity to sinicize the Islands of the Southwestern Pacific. The attempt of the pirate chieftain Li Ma-hong to capture Manila a century and a half later was not supported by the authorities in Peking.

Filipinos became most intimately part of the Malay world that centers around its own tropical Mediterranean following the rise of the Sri Vijayan empire on Sumatra in the eighth century. The Cailendra Dynasty, controlling the two vital entrances to these sheltered waters, the Straits of Malacca and Sunda, mustered wealth that supported the flowering of this Indo-Malay civilization. When the center of power was transferred to Java in 1292 with the supremacy of Majapahit rule, this emphasis upon an empire bound together around the seas continued. The Philippines were not formally conquered by these empires, although individual princes made forays into the Islands and some settled there with their followers. But Filipinos in the maritime communities which touched the periphery of these major civilizations felt

35

their cultural impact. In legend today Filipinos still link themselves to that distant and heroic era, lending added impulse to the sense of identity with their neighbors to the south and west. Then Islam in the fourteenth and fifteenth centuries spread through the Malay orbit and reached Luzon, marking its farthest advance in the Pacific. But the Muslim hold on the settled regions of the Philippines was tenuous, except for the most intensive areas of missionary effort in Mindanao and Sulu. They were handicapped also by their failure to form a centralized political structure such as fostered Islam in the lands of its early evolution. These followers of the Prophet were not afforded time to consolidate themselves in the Islands before they were challenged by the proponents of another vigorous, proselytizing faith.

Filipinos have experienced several abrupt breaks with their past history and one such fundamental change occurred when the Spanish *conquistadores* arrived in the Islands in the sixteenth century. Rivalry with Portugal for access to the riches derived from the spice trade with the East Indies encouraged the Spanish crown to send Ferdinand Magellan on the venture that led him around Cape Horn and across the Pacific to land in the Philippines in the spring of 1521. Actually, the Archipelago was then known as the St. Lazarus Islands and was given its present name in honor of Philip II, King of Spain. Magellan lost his life on Mactan Island near Cebu when he intervened in a feud between two local chieftains. But one of the ships in his fleet continued on west around Africa to Spain, completing the first recorded circumnavigation of the globe and arousing the interest of the Spanish monarchy in these distant islands that promised both access to the riches of the Moluccas and stepping stones to China. It remained for Miguel Lopez de Legaspi and his intrepid band of followers to initiate in 1561 the actual Spanish conquest of the Islands. With judicious foresight the Spanish crown had cautioned against an outright military subjugation of the Filipinos. Instead, these "soldiers of the cross and the sword" courted one local chieftain after the next, employing force where necessary but often using persuasion and taking advantage of rivalry between communities to gain their acceptance of Spanish sovereignty. Within some twenty years this policy of penetration enabled Spain to establish control over the major inhabited lowland regions, except for the strongly Muslim areas of Mindanao and Sulu.

From the outset Spain's leaders saw her role in the Islands as one devoted to far more worthy objectives than simply the search for wealth and real estate to add to her empire. It was a time when Spain felt herself to be the appointed protector of the Catholic

37

Church and the chosen instrument to extend the Christian faith, as she already had done in Mexico and elsewhere in the Americas. When the adventurers failed to find ready fortunes of gold in the Philippines and proposed to abandon the Islands, it was this sense of a holy mission and pride that induced the Spanish crown to insist upon retaining its new domain. Although administration of the Islands over many years represented a cash drain paid in silver coin from the coffers of the viceroy of Mexico, under whose jurisdiction the Philippines was placed, the authorities in Madrid never were diverted from this missionary policy.

As a consequence of this vision of her role, Spain's representatives in the Islands made conversion to Christianity through baptism the symbol of allegiance to the new authority. Initially, it was a fairly rough-handed matter with a chieftain and his followers accepting the new faith *en masse,* although they understood little concerning its meaning. The first Spanish soldiers in the Islands awarded *encomiendas* from which to collect taxes and exact labor also were haphazard in fulfilling their commitment to attend the spiritual welfare of their charges. Beginning with the first five Augustinian priests who arrived with Legaspi, however, the Catholic clergy took most seriously this responsibility. They always were handicapped for lack of more competently trained priests; it was a costly

38

and discouraging journey requiring often two years to send a missionary from Spain across Mexico and via the Pacific to the Philippines. And by 1655 when over 500,000 Filipinos had accepted Spanish authority there were only 60 secular priests and 254 regulars of the missionary orders in the Islands.

The extraordinary accomplishments of these Christian missionaries in transforming the landscape of the Philippines and the life of the people traced in part to the character of the native religious institutions they encountered. Among Filipinos who came under Spanish authority Islam was little more than a veneer superimposed upon earlier practices. Filipinos of this former persuasion placed their faith in a world of spirits, sometimes termed *anitos,* that might inhabit trees, rocks, or a marshy site. They were influences that the inhabitants sought to propitiate in an effort to ward off evil or secure healing of illness. Although the inhabitants had not constructed religious edifices, they did use groves of trees and caves as holy places. There was no systematized ritual of organized worship, even though Filipinos accepted the concept of an after-life. Elderly women usually were entrusted by the Islanders with the management of religious affairs. But they did not compose a tightly organized priesthood that saw itself challenged and was able to mobilize group resistance. Where a different pattern of religious leadership prevailed, as among the Moros

39

of Sulu and Mindanao and the Ifugaos and other tribal folk in the mountains of Northern Luzon, Christianity was able to make but scant inroads.

While the Spanish pioneer missionary-priest might make only superficial progress instructing the chieftains and nobles of the former society in the essentials of Christianity, he countered by schooling the children and winning the women. He also was helped by a conviction that grew among Filipinos who came to believe that the act of baptism afforded healing from illness; to this day many Filipinos still place trust in relief from physical suffering through worship. The pageantry that the Catholic Church introduced appealed mightily to the people. And the priests wisely incorporated earlier social customs into their religious observances. The practice can be observed today in the annual fiestas of each *barrio* or village when the special patron saint of the community is publicly honored.

Along with the teachings of the Bible the priests also introduced western practices. Leading Filipino families adopted Spanish dress, particularly for festive occasions. As they learned to speak Spanish they also acquired a taste for European cooking and Western-inspired furnishings for their homes. Spanish family surnames were assumed later; often they were taken from the Madrid tax lists. And the social ideal became the *ilustrado*, or gentleman of letters and leisure.

The physical handiwork of the priests can be seen in the spacious plazas they planned. Along the "king's road," often laid out to parallel the seashore, these sites were platted to take advantage of natural vistas. Massive stone churches, usually patterned upon European baroque architecture, were constructed to face the plaza, and less imposing religious and official buildings were grouped around. Compulsions were employed to secure labor, such as the requirement that each family bring its quota of building blocks to mass every Sunday, and these were often resented. But in time these plazas also became the centers of political and commercial life in municipalities throughout the Islands and are comparable today to the square in front of the American county court house. Each *barrio* aspires to its miniature duplicate of this arrangement, which also serves as a market place and center for community recreation. Since the shortage of clerics never permitted the church to staff every parish, priests were stationed as a rule in the municipal seat or *población* and periodically visited smaller chapels in surrounding *barrios*.

Economically, the Filipinos remained primarily subsistence farmers and fishermen. In agriculture, however, the priests also made significant contributions. Corn, sweet potatoes, and tobacco were introduced from the Americas, as were several varieties of tropical fruits including the avocado. Irrigation was en-

41

couraged on a larger scale to supply a surplus of rice for sale to developing urban communities. Sugar cane was cultivated as a commercial crop and in the latter period of Spanish rule the Islands became important exporters of the dark brown *muscavado* that also contained the molasses. Coconut plantations were established as commercial enterprises with the priests sometimes serving as technical specialists in agriculture. Originally, the Spanish had hoped to find spices growing in the Philippines as they did in the Moluccas to the south. When these did not materialize they investigated the possibilities for commercial planting of cinnamon, nutmeg, and pepper. But the regions of Mindanao best suited to growing spices were plagued by Moro pirates and this industry never became a major commercial venture. Growing of cotton declined as imports of finished cloth from India and China were marketed.

In pre-Spanish times land had been held as communal property by the *barangays* with the privileged classes enjoying special benefits. With the introduction of the Spanish concept of property the former chieftain and noble families were able to solidify their position through becoming landowners. Centralized control of wealth also was fostered by the awarding of large royal land grants to favored families and religious orders. Following abandonment of the *encomiendas* there emerged a gentry class both Filipino

42

and *mestizo* in origin known as the *cacique*. They became the dominant social class in the provinces, often building imposing homes around the plaza of the *población*. The dependent groups who in pre-Spanish society frequently were bound by a system of debt-peonage requiring them to work for leading families of the barangay now found themselves as tenants whose fate depended largely upon decisions of the *cacique*.

While the priests worked in the provinces to Christianize and westernize the Filipinos there grew up in Manila a special merchant group—predominantly Spanish, but including *mestizos* and others—whose interests centered upon the galleon trade. The lucrative commerce afforded by this opportunity largely diverted attention of the authorities from the more tedious task of developing fisheries, plantations and other forms of rural wealth on the scale of the Dutch effort in Indonesia and British enterprise in Ceylon. Chinese silks and porcelains, jewels from Burma and India, East Indian spices, camphor wood from Formosa and ivory from Cambodia, all found a ready market in the new world of the Americas. And Manila became the entrepôt where these goods were assembled; through control both of the Philippines and the west coast of the Americas from California to Cape Horn the Spanish were able to maintain for long a near monopoly for this galleon trade. The ships usu-

43

ally were constructed with timber taken from the forests surrounding Manila Bay, individual merchants and religious organizations paying for the cost of building the vessel by buying space. Annually, one or several such galleons sailed from Manila, and, following the Japan current north and east across the Pacific, docked at Acapulco on the lower western coast of Mexico, where the goods were transshipped. On the return journey west near the equator the vessels brought back the silver dollars in such demand throughout the Orient. It was a hazardous business as these simple sailing craft braved the fury of the Pacific storms, and merchants in Manila had to wait for many months to learn if they had made or lost a fortune. Entrepreneurs also risked having their galleons seized by British privateers like Sir Francis Drake, in this era when England was challenging Spain for control of the seas. But the galleon was the one physical tie that linked the Philippines to Mexico and ultimately to Spain; only after Mexico's independence in 1819 did regular commerce develop directly with Spain. It is one of the ironies of history that throughout more than two centuries of managing this galleon trade Spanish seamen never discovered the Hawaiian Islands, although such knowledge could have spared them much of the hardship of the trans-Pacific voyages.

The galleon trade drew to Manila numerous Chinese who annually brought the junks laden with valuable cargo. When the Spanish forces of Martín de Goiti first occupied Manila in 1571 they found some 60 Chinese families in residence. By 1596 the Spanish authorities had deported 12,000 Chinese from Manila and recorded that as many more remained. Officially, the Chinese were restricted to living in a ghetto-like *parian* up the Pasig River from the walled city of Manila but within easy reach of the guns on the Spanish stone forts. Those who remained behind when their junks sailed home were subject to special license fees and head taxes. As the Chinese population, including carpenters, shipwrights, artisans and merchants, multiplied rapidly, the Spanish authorities became fearful. Suspicion and intrigue heightened by rumors that the emperor of China was sending a force to seize the Philippines prompted the Spanish to engineer a massacre in 1603 that cost the lives of some 23,000 Chinese. But destruction of the Chinese community brought disaster to the galleon trade and soon the Spanish governor sent an envoy to Canton and invited the junks to come again. Such systematic though smaller massacres of the Chinese, motivated in part by the desire of some Spanish merchants to erase old debts, were repeated several times during the next century and a half. In time the authorities in Manila evolved more humane methods such as quotas and annual levies for curbing the Chinese. But an attitude toward the Chinese had been stamped upon the Filipino mind, making far more difficult the absorption of these thrifty, energetic and competent aliens who fulfill such vital economic functions.

The once creative role of Spain and the Catholic Church in the Philippines changed for the worse late in the seventeenth and early in the eighteenth century; it was aggravated by increasingly bitter conflict between church and state authorities in the Islands. Despite a brief and abortive effort at reform before and after the British occupation of Manila from 1762 to 1764, this decline continued. It was a time of decay for the far-flung Spanish empire. And as the resources available to support the administration in the Islands dwindled, both the civil authorities and the church became more self-seeking. Gone also was much of that conviction of a holy mission that had led the first Spanish representatives to view their role as one of liberating Filipinos from the "influences of the devil." Since the Philippines was at the very end of Spain's political lifeline the Islands suffered first and most, sometimes from "dumping" there of officials and priests unwanted elsewhere and also from outright neglect. As the Spanish civilian and military authorities sought to eliminate the priests from participation in provincial administration, the religious orders became increasingly occupied with managing their landed estates upon which they depended for support. In his role as an *hacendero* the priest veered from being a protector of the people and sometimes became a hardened exploiter. The corruption of the clergy that did so much to discredit the Church in the mind of a latter generation of Filipinos dates primarily from this time. And the reluctance of the religious orders to train and promote Filipino priests began to tell.

Opening of the port of Manila to world trade in 1837 ended the economic stagnation resulting from Spain's earlier monopolistic policies and brought sudden prosperity to owners of the large landed estates and the merchants. Manila hemp for rope became an internationally known commodity. Until it was wiped out by blight, coffee brought fortunes to some planters, particularly in Batangas. Sugar exports multiplied and created wealthy planter families in Negros, Panay, and Luzon. With income derived from this prosperity the more privileged Filipino families for the first time were able to educate their sons abroad. Particularly in Europe they were stirred by the new ideals of liberalism, the nineteenth century concern for science and enlightenment, that had hardly penetrated to the Philippines. Letters and journals mailed home awakened a new curiosity among the educated elite in the Islands. Books became cheaper and more readily available and the arts began to flourish. When the young men returned from their foreign schooling they helped lead a generation impatient for change. Filipinos who guided this movement, men like A. Mabini, Pardo de Tavera, León Ma. Guerrero, Isabelo de Los Reyes, the Luna Brothers, and many others, often were scholars, artists, and professionally gifted as well as political agitators. From Europe they borrowed ideas of organization that resulted in the Masonic movement, aimed at curbing the Church, and secret societies propagandizing their fellow Filipinos with concepts of individual freedom and democratic rights.

Instead of accommodating itself to these new trends, the Spanish administration in Manila resorted to repression—this reaction became particularly severe when the monarchy was restored at Madrid in 1871. Successive earlier revolts against alien rule had been localized, although resistance had continued for many years in outlying regions such as the Island of Bohol. But now a new sense of national identity fortified Filipino determination to share more fully in the management of their birthright. Discontent led to a mutiny of Filipino troops stationed at Cavite. It was poorly organized and soon suppressed by the Spanish authorities; forty-one of the mutineers were executed and widespread arrest of civilians followed. Three Filipino priests who had demanded equal opportunities with the European clergy lost their lives for this in 1872 and this fostered further dissension within the Church. Sixteen years later resentment against the friars as owners of rich lands who also controlled much local administration sparked a massive popular demonstration and a petition to the Spanish Crown for their withdrawal.

Demands of the intellectuals for liberty now aroused less privileged Filipinos to seek social justice. In 1892 Andres Bonifacio and his comrades founded the Katipunan as a secret revolutionary society with a mass appeal. For nearly four years they quietly enlisted members, printed propaganda and organized. When existence of the Katipunan was discovered by the Spanish authorities, they initiated a reign of terror. Bonifacio and his fellow leaders fled to the provinces and in August of 1896 launched an armed revolt that soon spread from Ilocos through Cavite to Batangas and later was joined by Filipinos in Cebu. But the rebels were weakened by internal dissension and the movement lost much of its impetus when Bonifacio was executed, allegedly upon instructions of the revolutionary council. Emilio Aguinaldo emerged as the strongest of the insurgent leaders and continued the struggle into the following year. As they were driven back into the hills, however, the rebels lost confidence. Faced with dwindling support, General Aguinaldo and his associates accepted a Spanish offer of safe conduct to Hongkong and payment there of 600,000 *pesos* in return for calling off the rebellion. Failure of their revolution served chiefly to embitter the younger generation of Filipinos and fostered the spirit of inde-

49

pendence that later found expression in the Republic established at Malolos.

It was during this time of turmoil that José Rizal emerged as a symbol of Filipino creativeness at its best. Extraordinarily gifted from youth, imbued with a vital concern for freedom by his mother's unjust imprisonment and schooled by the Jesuits, he was foremost among Filipinos who studied abroad. All that he learned from association with European scholars helped give him an image of the potential greatness of his own people. His novels of passionate social protest, *Noli Me Tangere* and *El Filibusterismo,* and numerous other writings stirred Filipinos at home. Rizal wrote in Spanish and was as much European as Asian. He was also a "renaissance man," broadly talented as a doctor, sculptor and thinker. His organization of La Liga Filipina in 1892 was equally concerned with regenerating his people and compelling the Spanish to institute reforms. Although opposed to violence, Rizal was charged with complicity in the revolt and was executed on December 30, 1896. As a martyr he has become the greatest national hero and a model for many idealistic young men and women in the Islands.

## 3. The Philippines Under the Stars and Stripes

Filipinos are equally heirs to a second great missionary enterprise: United States efforts to foster in the Islands institutions of government and attitudes toward life derived from American experience and faith in democratic ways. The Philippines was acquired in 1898 at the Treaty of Paris that closed the Spanish-American War, and for nearly half a century this occupation marked the one great and avowed U. S. "adventure in imperialism." Today, citizens of the Republic are intimately linked in taste, as in politics and respect for freedom of the individual, by this association. At least among Asians, American professions of intent and capacity to help emerging new nations are judged in part by U. S.

performance in the Islands. The future course of events in the Western Pacific and Southeastern Asia depends substantially upon the quality of Philippine-American cooperation; presence in the Islands of the large U. S. military bases that anchor the democratic defense shield extending from Formosa to Bangkok is one manifestation of this vital relationship.

Formal advent of the United States onto the Philippine scene dates from the morning of May 1, 1898, when Commodore George Dewey's fewer but more heavily armed naval vessels destroyed the Spanish squadron in Manila Bay. War with Spain had been precipitated by the sinking of the U. S. battleship *Maine,* reportedly by an exterior mine, in Havana Harbor in February of that year. Sometime before, however, the American public had become aroused by the Cuban struggle against Spanish rule. Younger men active in the administration in Washington, D. C., such as Assistant Secretary of the Navy Theodore Roosevelt, became convinced that the remaining Spanish empire was disintegrating. Unless the U. S. acted, they feared that more modern European powers would move into the vacuum. Prior to the outbreak of war and before proceeding to take command of the U. S. Asiatic squadron, Commodore Dewey had made an intensive study of the charts of Philippine waters and his naval vessels were in a high state of readiness for the opportunity afforded by hostilities.

52

Just as had been done in Cuba, the U. S. followed the outbreak of war by encouraging and arming Filipino insurgent forces. General Emilio Aguinaldo, strongest among the military leaders of the abortive 1896 revolt, was en route to Europe when he was intercepted aboard ship in Singapore by the U. S. Consul and induced to return to Hongkong. Aguinaldo was picked up in the British colony by one of Dewey's ships, placed ashore in Cavite, given arms and encouraged to organize Filipinos. Resentment against continued Spanish abuses evoked a prompt response to this new revolutionary appeal and Spain's defeat and demoralization of her forces soon enabled Filipino irregulars to capture much of the countryside. Following American occupation of Manila, however, differences developed between the U. S. authorities and Filipino leaders. The Filipinos insisted they simply wanted the U. S. to help in ousting Spain and leave them to establish an independent government. In pursuit of this objective, Filipino revolutionary leaders held a constitutional convention at Malolos, organizing a government of their own that soon claimed substantial jurisdiction, particularly on Luzon.

The United States was caught in a dilemma compounded somewhat of its own mixed motives. The prospects of Filipinos retaining their independence did not appear to be good in the face of the obvious interest of the Germans, who then had naval vessels

53

anchored in Manila Bay, and also of the Japanese. In the United States there were potent groups who felt the U. S. had defeated Spain and should rightly be successors to sovereignty. Accidental hostilities then erupted between Filipino revolutionary forces and U. S. troops occupying Manila and environs and this prompted an American decision to pacify the Islands by military means. The U. S. fought a campaign that was encouraged to a degree by Filipinos who felt they were not ready to stand on their own, and which terminated with the capture of General Aguinaldo and his headquarters. This action of extending American jurisdiction by force, however, aroused many doubts and much heated debate in the United States. Liberal leaders in America, particularly in the Democratic Party, then in opposition, made the Philippines an issue in domestic politics for several presidential election campaigns.

The administration of President William McKinley responded with a compromise solution; they would keep the Philippines under the American flag but with the purpose of protecting them and preparing the people for democratic self-government. This objective in time enlisted some of the best talents the U. S. had to offer. Instructions issued to the second Philippine Commission that established civil government in the Islands on July 4, 1901, offer the most concise guide to the character of the effort:

54

"In all forms of government and administrative provisions which they are authorized to prescribe, the Commission should bear in mind that the government which they are establishing is designed not for our satisfaction or for the expression of our theoretical views, but for the happiness, peace and prosperity of the people of the Philippine Islands, and the measures adopted should be made to conform to their customs, their habits and even their prejudices, to the fullest extent consistent with the accomplishment of the indispensable requisites of just and effective government. At the same time the Commission should bear in mind, and the people of the Islands should be made plainly to understand, that there are certain great principles of government which have been made the basis of our governmental system, which we deem essential to the rule of law and the maintenance of individual freedom, and of which they have, unfortunately, been denied the experience possessed by us; that there are also certain practical rules of government which we have found essential to the preservation of these great principles of liberty and law, and that these principles and these rules of government must be established and maintained in their islands for the sake of their liberty and happiness, however much they may conflict with the customs or laws of procedure with which they are familiar."

The American effort in the Islands, however, only

succeeded because from the outset it enjoyed the support of a large portion of the better informed and more publicly conscious Filipinos. Three such Filipinos served on the Commission with the first civil governor, William Howard Taft, and in this capacity shared in deliberations of policy and their execution. Although the first supreme court appointed under the U. S. administration included a majority of Americans, the chief justice was a Filipino. Filipinos helped frame the new legal system that retained much Spanish substantive law but introduced American procedural law better to safeguard individual rights. Some among the Spanish-educated elite remained hostile to the new and predominantly Protestant administration that was upsetting the former social system which afforded substantial privileges for the few. Also, some Filipino revolutionary leaders were reluctant to accept postponement of independence or doubted America's ultimate intentions. But the influence of both groups dwindled as they were identified more with the past than the future.

The administration now developed for the Archipelago became a model for its time. Americans who joined in this enterprise were imbued with enthusiasm and energy; conviction that they were bringing the blessings of democracy to a deserving people lent a sense of moral rightness. Once peace and order were established with the help of a locally recruited Philippine Constabulary, first attention was given to public health. Disorganization following disturbances of war had spread disease, and several cholera epidemics took a fearful toll, in some years causing a net reduction in population. Now the U. S. Army joined in digging wells, installing sewage systems and otherwise modernizing city sanitation. Army engineer units planned and built highways and bridges; the present mountain road up to the summer capital in Baguio a mile above sea level is among the monuments to their efforts. The *peso* was stabilized at a value of two for one dollar and weights and measures standardized with official adoption of the metric system.

Among the U. S. administrators were able men who found career opportunities circumscribed at home and were excited by the challenge of creating a Philippine civil service emphasizing merit. Such men established the Bureau of Printing, the Bureau of Forestry, a Bureau of Fisheries and the Customs Service. They were aided by able persons on the scene like the Jesuit scientist, José Algué, who founded the Weather Bureau and pioneered in seismology. In the new Bureaus of Agriculture, Science, and Mining they organized systematic research to explore natural resources in the Archipelago. Although whalers from New England had fished in Philippine waters early in the nineteenth century and a few merchants and scholars had visited there, U. S. knowledge of its new domain was sketchy

57

when the forces arrived. Now a special Bureau of Non-Christian Tribes was organized, staffed in part by ethnologists and anthropologists who initiated systematic investigation of these peoples that had remained isolated and virtually unknown during the Spanish era. In the Sulu Archipelago and Mindanao the U. S. encountered the same fierce opposition from Muslim Moros that had denied Spanish control over the region. Moro *datus* refused to let their children be educated, fearing this would mean conversion to Christianity. Instead, a *datu* might send a younger slave to study. In dealing with these determined local chieftains the U. S. employed a combination of persuasion and force. General of the Armies John J. Pershing first distinguished himself as a captain fighting the Moro *datus* around Lake Lanao. It was a slow process, and for many years the Department of Mindanao and Sulu remained a special responsibility of the U. S. Army.

Introduction of a public school system employing English for instruction proved the most consequential of all American innovations. Prior to this time education had been the privilege of the few who could afford to send their children to schools managed by the religious orders. Now soldiers were recruited to become teachers. Soon they were followed by "Thomasites," so named for the U. S. Army transport that brought to Manila the largest contingent of these teachers selected by civil service examination. More than 1,000 such teachers went into the provinces to open schools. As Filipino teachers were trained and joined them, enrollment in public elementary and high schools multiplied. The 150,000 students in schools as of 1900 increased to more than 1,000,000 in 1921 and to over 2,000,000 by 1940; a figure that was to triple during the next two decades. Vocational schools and normal schools to train educational personnel were opened. And as had been the case in rural America, the teacher became an honored citizen of the community where he or she taught.

Filipinos, initially puzzled by all this American concern with education, appreciated its value when they saw graduates given opportunity under the new administration. Schooling for their sons and daughters soon became the foremost ambition of most Filipino families and remains to this day a major national motivation. Textbooks first came direct from American school systems and young Filipinos read about George Washington, Benjamin Franklin, Thomas Jefferson and Abraham Lincoln, and learned to recite their speeches. They also imbibed a new sense of values as they saw how a man of humble origins could rise through his own efforts. The establishment of a national University of the Philippines afforded training in leadership, encouraging a new type of Filipino, a man with access to the accumulated learning of the

English-speaking world and moved by its emphasis upon science and liberal thought.

The Catholic Church, so dominant during the Spanish era, now experienced its own metamorphosis. Revolt against Spain had stirred some Filipino members of the clergy to join in creation of a Philippine Independent Church that severed all ties with Rome and competed for a following. U. S. administration opened the Islands to Protestant missionaries who soon gained a small but important membership for their churches, particularly among the emerging middle class. Confronted with this challenge and spurred by reports coming from Catholic U. S. Army chaplains who cited abuses by the priests, the Church acted. Some hundreds of Spanish priests were recalled from the Islands. They often were replaced by American Catholics more in harmony with the new administration. Governor Taft arranged for the U. S. Congress to vote a special bond issue to purchase the friar estates and resell them to Filipinos, thereby sparing the Church the onus of being a major rural land owner and partially solving a festering social problem. Although the Church still had to contend with fierce anti-clericalism of many Filipinos active in the independence movement or suspicious of Rome, most Catholic institutions survived the transition and prospered under the new order.

Among all the American introductions none proved

more congenial for Filipinos than the new profession of politics. By act of the U. S. Congress elective government was instituted in the municipalities in 1902, extending the restricted franchise of the Spanish period. The Philippine Assembly, created in 1907, was an elected national lower house and opened opportunities for a new type of leadership; Filipinos now depended for influence and status primarily upon their capacity to win votes rather than on possession of wealth. Although *cacique* families often controlled this rising generation of "talkers" by financing their campaigns or marrying their daughters to such men of promise, a leaven was at work. To attract a following the rising Filipino politician was compelled to cater to popular aspirations, although he did not involve himself too deeply with critical issues. From such origins emerged Manuel Quezon, Sergio Osmeña and a generation of men with like spirit who began to mold and use public opinion.

President Woodrow Wilson's administration brought a major change in American management of the Philippines. For years the Democrats had belabored the Republicans over their "imperial venture" in the Islands. Fragmentary evidence suggests that President Wilson originally planned to give the Philippines prompt independence. Apparently, he was dissuaded from this by the outbreak of World War I. Instead, the U. S. proceeded to "Filipinize" the administration

61

and many able American civil servants in the Islands were replaced by Filipinos; during Wilson's two terms in office, Americans in the Insular Government were reduced from 2,600 to 582. More consequential was the Jones Act, passed by the U. S. Congress in 1916. It provided for election of a Philippine Senate and afforded Filipinos in their Congress primary control over fiscal policy. However, Wilsonian liberalism, aimed at fostering more democratic institutions, defeated some of its own objectives. Few Filipinos yet had risen from the ranks of the majority of citizens and qualified themselves to take advantage of the new opportunities. As a consequence, social groups dominant during the Spanish era were able to regain a decisive hold upon Philippine affairs.

The Philippine independence movement during the American period never became the bitter and sometimes bloody struggle that led proponents of self-rule to revolt or to prison under many colonial regimes in Asia. Rather, the champions of the "Philippines to be run by Filipinos" usually employed this cause as a political platform that won them a following and national prominence. The hallmark of political success was to lead a mission to Washington, D. C. and, by publicity and persuasion, win concessions from the U. S. Congress and the White House. (In the process, Filipinos became adept at playing off one American political faction against the other and soon discovered the foibles of U. S. senators that could be employed to the advantage of their cause.) Nor was there resentment against the "whites," so often found in colonial lands. Intermarriage among Filipinos and foreigners was far more frequent and acceptable than elsewhere in Asia, and lack of a "color line" spared the Philippines that ill feeling. Development of an alien landholding class and acquisition of large tracts by American corporations were deliberately discouraged by both the U. S. Congress and the Insular Government. And Filipinos soon learned that they could outwit their rulers in business as in politics. Overcompensation for once injured national pride is not a common Filipino trait and they are able to treat Americans and others as equals. They learned to look with scorn upon foreigners who would be "carpet-baggers" and generally accepted with friendly hospitality those who came to make their homes in the Islands. This maturity enabled Filipinos to accord genuine respect to some truly able Americans and other Westerners who dedicated the better years of their lives to furthering progress in the Philippines.

The formal terms of independence were spelled out in the Tydings-McDuffie Act passed by the U. S. Congress in 1934; the Philippines was to become a self-governing Commonwealth under the American flag for ten years before achieving total independence. A constitutional convention meeting in Manila in 1934–35 framed a government with an executive, legislative and judicial structure similar to that of the United States. A fourth branch of government was added in 1940 with creation of the Commission on Elections as an independent body to supervise the electoral contests scheduled every two years—Philippine elections are held every other odd year on the second Tuesday of November, as contrasted to American national elections held during even years. Manuel Quezon, who emerged as the dominant figure of the independence movement, was elected the first president of the Commonwealth; though he demonstrated but limited concern for improving the lot of the ordinary *tao* or farmer, he was a gifted master of the new political process.

The decision to grant the Philippines independence at this time was among the early moves of the first administration of President Franklin D. Roosevelt; it contrasted with the previous twelve years of Republican attention to improving administrative quality in the Insular Government following a decline coincident with earlier "Filipinization." But the grant to Filipinos of complete jurisdiction over their own affairs was prompted as much by American domestic economic pressure groups as by liberal views in Washington, D. C. and the U. S. "anti-colonial conscience." The Payne Tariff Act of 1909 had established near free trade between the Philippines and the United

States; export industries in the Islands had profited, as had the market for American manufacturers. The Philippines became the world's largest coconut producing nation, meeting demands of the growing U. S. soap and other oil industries. Hemp and tobacco growing was expanded. During and after World War I the Insular Government encouraged the building of modern sugar centrals or mills and by the early 1930's annual production reached nearly 1,500,000 tons. The first sugar act of the U. S. Congress in 1934 restricted the Islands to providing 14 percent of American consumption, or 952,000 tons yearly. At the depth of the depression, American domestic and Cuban producers of sugar and oil crops saw in independence for Filipinos an opportunity to curtail competition from these imports; Filipino leaders were quick to capitalize upon this powerful impetus to their cause.

Just as they were preparing the enjoy the heady experience of independence, the outbreak of World War II in the Pacific brought Filipinos another kind of foreign domination that led many to question the viability of a small new country on its own. While costing the Philippines terribly in loss of life and physical destruction, the war also fostered a vast social reshuffle. Old patterns of privilege were upset and opportunities afforded through the resistance movement for younger men of energy and competence to rise. The struggle also left a heritage of "moral anarchy" that continues

65

to plague the Islands. General of the Army Douglas MacArthur, who was in command of Philippine defenses following inauguration of the Commonwealth, had assured Filipinos that they were protected against all enemies; this lulled them into an unreal sense of security during the opening years of this global conflict in China and Europe. It was a shock to Filipinos when, following the bombing of the U. S. Pacific Fleet at Pearl Harbor, the Imperial Japanese forces invaded Luzon, landing at Lingayen Gulf, Aparri in the north, Lamon Bay on the east and elsewhere. After the original plan to defend the Philippines "on the beaches" was abandoned and the U. S.-Philippine forces withdrew into the Bataan Peninsula and the rock fortress of Corregidor, the spectacle of disaster overwhelmed some leaders. President Quezon considered an appeal to declare the Commonwealth neutral. He was induced to forego such action and with Vice-President Sergio Osmeña and a few of their staff evacuated to Australia. The months of bitter battle delayed the Japanese military timetable for an advance through the Southwest Pacific to Australia, but the defenders were doomed. The Filipino and American troops were green and ill-prepared for such combat with the exception of the Philippine Scouts who formed an integral and professional component of the U. S. Army. The supplies of food stockpiled in the jungle fortress on Bataan were inadequate, for huge quantities of rice and flour had been abandoned in the withdrawal from other sections of Luzon; malnutrition and disease took a tragic toll. After the surrender of the Phil-American forces on Bataan the fall of Corregidor was only a matter of time, as Japanese artillery and bombing blanketed this guardian post at the entrance to Manila Bay. The "Death March," when allied survivors of Bataan were driven north to the concentration camp at Capas and O'Donnell, was a final humiliation that the Japanese imposed on their foes, partly intended to denigrate Americans in Filipino eyes.

The Japanese, bolstered by their victories over the British in Hongkong, Malaya, Singapore and Burma, and the Dutch in Indonesia, now sought to incorporate the Philippines in their "Greater East Asia Co-Prosperity Sphere." Initially, the Japanese planned to be welcomed as liberators and made some corresponding concessions. Filipinos captured while fighting with U. S. forces were released from prison. There were pronouncements about "Asia for the Asiatics" and efforts to identify Japan with the earlier Philippine revolutionary movement. Independence for the Islands was proclaimed in 1943 and a government established under Japanese protection and supervision. Some leading Filipinos joined this government, seeing it as an opportunity for protecting their people from the harsher features of Japanese occupation. Others were "trimmers," anxious to safeguard their own or family interests. However, the Japanese Army soon offended and angered Filipinos. Soldiers of the emperor often seized chickens and pigs without payment, bathed naked in the streets, slapped Filipinos who failed to show respect and in time resorted to ruthless torture and killing of civilians. This contrasted with the regard for legal rights of the individual so characteristic of the American administration. Indignation at such trampling upon their freedom combined with real loyalty to the democratic cause sent ever more Filipinos to join guerrillas in the resistance. These irregular forces, sometimes supplied from Australia, multiplied rapidly. They harassed and sabotaged the Japanese and collected information. Filipino collaborators were hunted down. Occasionally, a guerrilla chieftain set himself up as a local potentate and sought to settle old feuds by force or to eliminate potential post-war business competitors. But out of this resistance movement came new Filipino leaders, tested in the hard school of command decisions, gifted at organization and skilled in effective action. They came from all strata of society, for birth and wealth no longer offered assurances of advantage, and they were to provide vitality for democratic institutions.

When U. S. and other allied forces that had fought their way up from the Solomons and New Guinea returned to Leyte, Samar, and Luzon in 1944–45, they were welcomed as true liberators. During the days

68

leading to their final defeat, Japanese commanders in gestures of bitter vengeance burned schools, churches, and public buildings. Thousands of innocent civilians were executed, occasionally without any formal charges. The contrast with the American G.I.'s, who shared their candy, clothes, and rations, left an indelible impression. So did the discovery by Filipinos in the barrios that they could drink, fight, and make friends with Americans in uniform. In the last months of the war on Luzon thousands of Filipinos—many of them boys in their teens—joined regular U. S. and Philippine forces to fight the enemy through the mountains, often without pay. Along the way they acquired a taste for chewing gum and travel by jeep and a mastery of picturesque G.I. phrases.

This first postwar era was a rough and unruly time, when much of the land lay in ruins—Greater Manila was fought over with the full fury of Japanese and U. S. military might and emerged a smoking ruin, more thoroughly destroyed than any capital in the world except Warsaw. Wartime shortages of food, medicine, and clothing generated appetites that tempted to theft and fast dealing. Destruction of most official records left scant evidence of who was entitled to what. It is one of the blemishes on the record of the U. S. Army that in this period when decisions were so consequential some among its officers showed miserable judgment in according guerrilla recognition. Often it was an individual whose wartime record consisted chiefly of sitting around Manila cafes and whispering his dislike of the enemy or doing "buy and sell" who gained the ear of a confused American major and was accredited as a resistance veteran, with all of the attendant status, back pay, and G.I. benefits. When the real fighters came in out of the jungles only a portion were recognized and many proven patriots were denied this prized appreciation of their services. Many years after the war no single issue causes such deep personal grievance in Philippine-American relations as the injustice done some Filipinos who did give of their best in joint liberation of their homeland.

## 4.  The Free Philippines

Formal withdrawal of U. S. sovereignty over the
Islands came on July 4, 1946, as the Philippines was
proclaimed a fully independent republic. Shattering
experiences of the war had raised many doubts about
the viability of independence in an uncertain world and
some Filipino and American statesmen felt the date
for launching the Republic should be postponed until
the economy and public services were restored. But
most Filipino leaders had built political careers deeply
committed to independence and the authorities in
Washington, D. C., were anxious to present a clean
"Philippine record" to justify speeding self-government for other Asians under European colonial rule.
Consequently, the issue never was put to a direct vote
of all Filipinos, some of whom had mixed feelings on

71

this score, tempering the attractions of independence with a new awareness of its hazards.

Elections scheduled for the previous November were delayed due to continued postwar disorganization and scattered Japanese resistance. Instead, they were held in April, 1946. A split in the former coalition of political leaders led to the defeat of the Nacionalista Party headed by Commonwealth President Sergio Osmeña, who had succeeded to the office upon the wartime death of Quezon in the United States. Now a new Liberal Party emerged and captured control of the administration, electing Manuel Roxas as president and Elpidio Quirino as vice-president. It was they who took the oath of office on Independence Day on the grassy Luneta fronting on Manila Bay, not far from the spot where José Rizal had been executed. Several hundred thousand Filipinos crowded before the improvised grandstands and delegations from twenty-two foreign countries were on hand to inaugurate the new nation and to join in ceremonies that included the raising of the Philippine flag to replace the Stars and Stripes. Throughout the Islands each city and municipality held its own celebration; the parades, bands, speeches and salutes that Filipinos staged were not dissimilar from the ceremonies that mark the Fourth of July in the United States.

The new Republic hardly could have been launched under greater handicaps. The economy was at a near standstill. Japanese and guerrilla forces had bought or stolen and eaten a large proportion of the *carabaos* that farmers depended upon to till their fields. Seed grains that should have been saved for planting had been eaten, and rice mills, warehouses, and inter-island shipping were largely destroyed. Most sugar mills had been wrecked and the cane fields left idle or grown up to weeds. The hemp export industry had suffered from neglect, from the repatriation of the Japanese settlers who were among the largest of the pre-war growers, and from the substitution of other fibers in the world market. Coconut plantations had fared best, but many driers were burned and the trucks that formerly collected the copra at the ports for export rarely survived the struggle. The Filipino people had experienced nearly a million casualties and the survivors were weakened by malnutrition and disease. Malaria, which was eradicated before the war from most densely populated communities, now had returned to infest both old and young.

Dignitaries who assembled in Manila to observe the inauguration of the Republic looked out over a capital city whose ruins symbolized the wrecked public services of the new government. Japanese defenders had cemented themselves into the Houses of Congress, the City Hall, the Post Office and other once proud public buildings patterned upon the architecture of Washington, D. C., and been blasted out by the

73

U. S. Forces. Now the "Pearl of the Orient" with its former tree-shaded avenues, excellent sanitation facilities and blend of European and native architecture was 80 percent demolished, leaving the gaunt remains of shell-shattered concrete buildings and the skeletons of once massive cathedrals in the Spanish walled city. Government bureaus with their files and instruments had also become casualties of the conflict. Scientific collections, including the magnificent herbarium, were largely burned. Throughout the Islands, bridges, harbor installations and communications had been destroyed.

Another stumbling block in the way of recovery and united national action was the explosive issue of collaboration, over which Filipinos were bitterly divided. When Commonwealth President Quezon left Manila in 1941 with General of the Army MacArthur he had instructed the senior leaders remaining behind to act together in dealing with the occupying Japanese. The brunt of this unhappy task was borne by Jorge B. Vargas, as mayor of Greater Manila and chairman of the Executive Commission created by order of the Japanese military, and by José B. Laurel, who served as president of the puppet republic which Japan sponsored. But most of the older generation of political leaders including President Roxas had been associated with this enemy-supported government. Some Filipinos had made fortunes buying for the Japanese or speculating in scarce commodities, and "Mickey Mouse money" printed by the occupying power sometimes was used to purchase valuable property. There were plain citizens who found they only could survive these difficult times by becoming small merchants, and it was a rare individual who did not claim afterwards that he had secretly worked to aid the resistance, but such contentions were not easily evaluated.

Guerrilla leaders like Tomás Confesor of Panay and Tomás Cabili, the burly chieftain from Mindanao who became the first postwar Secretary of Defense, demanded an accounting. The United States, which could have exercised jurisdiction in the first liberation period, chose instead to leave this intricate problem for Filipinos to resolve. President Osmeña had induced the Philippine Congress to establish a People's Court to try those accused of collaboration. However, Solicitor General Lorenzo Tañada, another of the guerrilla leaders, and his staff encountered innumerable delays. The issue was officially closed when President Roxas, on January 28, 1948, declared a general amnesty for all but those found guilty of treason or of otherwise militarily aiding the Japanese. But for many years this issue influenced political decisions and served as a bond that united the younger postwar leaders in opposition to formerly dominant groups.

During the first postwar period Filipinos indulged in reckless spending, encouraged by pent-up desires for simple necessities such as shoes, or a can of milk for their children, and for luxuries they had missed during the hard years. U. S. aid and expenditures in the Philippines during the first five years of independence exceeded the value of $2,000,000,000. This included an appropriation of $520,000,000 by the U. S. Congress for private and public war damage payments; recognized private claimants were paid in full for the first $500 and thereafter 52 cents on each one dollar of 1941 valuation of their loss. Nearly $200,000,000 went to Filipino veterans for back pay and some $250,000,000 to civilian employees of the U. S. Army. Scattered throughout the Islands were enormous stockpiles of equipment including jeeps, trucks, bulldozers, uniforms, rations, medical supplies, and the like accumulated to support the planned invasion of Japan. This war materiel had cost well over $1,000,000,000 and now was transferred to the new government for a nominal value of $100,000,000. Capitalizing upon the opportunity to trade in such surplus goods and on the urgent needs of the economy, a class of Filipinos and Americans now emerged who frequently made quick fortunes.

The ensuing and perhaps inevitable moral corrosion left deep scars upon Filipino society. During the war it had become patriotic to steal from the enemy. Now individuals determined to help themselves or their families occasionally resorted to similar meth-

ods. Several Congressmen and Senators were prominent among those who flaunted their corruption. Consequently, the little man who could "get away with
it" tended to become at times a folk hero. In such an
atmosphere reestablishment of a civil service with the
excellent standards of the prewar period was extremely
difficult. Records had been lost, further complicating
the problem. As a result, the man seeking a position
in government did not attempt to advance through
merit but came to rely upon political patronage. Politicians could induce bureau chiefs to appoint their pro-
tégés by approving the "line item" budget in Congress.
Responsible leaders who recognized the dangers in
this system were compelled to join in the practice to
protect their own political careers. Inflation aggravated the problem—the price for rice was five times
that of prewar—and fostered a new mentality of
materialism that undermined respect for unselfish
public service.

It was in the hinterland, however, away from the
heady atmosphere of Manila's "get rich quick at any
price" environment, that the postwar distortion of national emphasis bred its most acute consequences. Particularly during the last decades before the war there
had been expressions of peasant discontent. Most no-
table was the Sakdal uprising of 1935. It was a quasi-
religious movement, like most mass efforts in Philippine history, but linked to politics and spurred by a

77

popular conviction among rural folk that they were entitled to a better deal. In the "rice granary" of Central Luzon and especially in Pampanga Province a socialist movement had been launched, aimed at redressing the abuse of tenants by some of their landlords and moneylenders. Although the Communists had begun during this period to seek converts to their cause, the Islands had not produced a radical political organization with a clear-cut economic program. The Japanese occupation prompted the Socialists and Communists to join in creating the "Anti-Japanese Peoples Liberation Army," that became popularly known as the *Hukbalahap*. With characteristic adroitness the Communists managed indoctrination of tenant farmers that were recruited. From sheltered bases deep in the Candaba swamps of Central Luzon, among the fish ponds and marshes north of Manila along the Bay and hideouts in the Sierra Madre Mountains, they struck at the enemy while also building their strength and gathering arms. Old prewar grudges led to bloody feuds between the Huks and the "USAFFE" guerrilla forces that included some American officers and sons of several prominent gentry families.

Disaster might have been averted had the guerrillas who fought with the Huks received recognition with back pay, if energetic attention had been paid to social reform and improved livelihood for them, and they had consequently been enabled to return to peace-

ful pursuits. Instead, the Huks found themselves faced
with the prospect of a marginal, humdrum way of
life that negated the exciting expectations generated
during the war, when the wealthy had sometimes to
seek food and protection from the poor. The problem
was compounded by the refusal of the Roxas administration to permit the seating of seven Congressmen
elected from Central Luzon with Huk support, including their *Supremo,* Luis Taruc; in part this was
aimed at assuring passage of the Parity Amendment
to the Constitution regulating the economic terms of
independence and according equal rights to U. S. citizens until 1974. The Huks still had their guns and,
bolstered by bitterness, they began mobilizing the peas-
antry for revolt. After President Elpidio Quirino succeeded to office in 1948 following the death of Roxas
there was a brief amnesty offer and attempts at a
peaceful solution. But mutual suspicion combined with
Communist determination to match the revolutionary
performance of their comrades in China and Southeast Asia led to a resumption of the rebellion.

The Philippine Republic came close to losing its
heritage of freedom during the next several years.
Army and constabulary units sent into the provinces
of Luzon to quell the Huks frequently abused the
people, sometimes shelling homes of innocent villagers
and bringing terror instead of protection. Large landowners organized and armed personal guard detach-

ments to enforce their will as well as security. The Rice Share Tenancy Act, designed to protect the peasant by guaranteeing him 70 percent of the crop when he supplied his own work animals, tools, and seed, regularly was ignored; *hacenderos* sometimes joined with local Constabulary commanders to insure collections of rents at the former rate of one-half of the crop. Loss of public confidence in legally constituted government was further aggravated by the presidential election of 1949. Officially, the Liberal Party headed by President Quirino was declared the winner, but actually there was some flagrant intimidation of candidates and voters and tampering with ballot boxes in several provinces. Followers of the defeated Nacionalista candidate, José Laurel, briefly took to the hills of Batangas threatening revolt, but were induced through negotiation to return home. During the election campaign administration candidates had freely distributed treasury warrants to pay for bridges and other improvements in communities where they sought votes. Now the national treasury proved unable to meet these and the salaries of teachers and some other national government employees fell three and four months in arrears. Construction of roads and other public works had to be halted for lack of funds. That same year the Philippine Government imposed exchange controls to husband its limited foreign reserves, providing opportunity for a new and more flagrant form of corruption and many quick fortunes in Manila.

Confronted with this mismanagement of independence and democracy at home, Filipinos in 1950 also saw their way of life threatened from without. Late the previous year the Red Armies had completed the conquest of mainland China. With the outbreak of the Korean War in June of 1950 it appeared that the Islands might soon again be engulfed in international conflict. This Filipino concern was matched by a belated U. S. reassessment of Philippine affairs, motivated in part by a new and more critical dependence upon the Republic for defense of the Western Pacific. The United States had retained substantial air, naval and other military bases in the Islands by terms of an agreement signed in 1947. Even these were threatened by the Huk revolt and the U. S. was compelled to use armed convoys to supply its 158,000-acre Clark Air Base-Fort Stotsenburg Reservation in Central Luzon. As some Filipinos began to doubt their capacity to manage a representative form of government, it became apparent elsewhere in Asia that the Philippine Republic, which the U. S. had sponsored as a model for independence, was not meeting the aspirations of its citizens.

After special economic and military missions had surveyed the Philippine problem in the summer of 1950, the U. S. arranged for an emergency loan to pay the Army, in the event that the national treasury defaulted on this obligation. A Joint U. S. Military Advisory Group was established on the outskirts of Manila, including among its complement of several dozen officers a few men of rare talent. With the appointment of Ramón Magsaysay as Secretary of Defense a thorough reorganization of the Armed Forces of the Philippines was initiated. A man of extraordinary energy and rare personal magnetism, he had risen through the guerrilla movement to become military governor of his home province, Zambales, and served in Congress on the Armed Forces Committee of the House. Now, with the assistance of other former guerrilla leaders who were brought back into uniform, staff study groups were created to design a new type of army; selected senior officers were retired to make room for these vigorous younger men.

A new military concept, relying on both force and persuasion, was now applied to combat the Huk revolt and to make the army a genuine protector of the people. The regular forces were recast around battalion combat teams numbering some 1,200 men each; one such unit also fought with United Nations troops in Korea. Formerly, the Army had confined its activities largely to the towns and regions near the highways. Now these combat teams hunted the Huks in their jungle and mountain hideouts. Magsaysay often joined his men, traveling by jeep, plane, or on foot to make surprise inspections. Military courtesy in dealings with civilians was rigidly enforced among soldiers, and they were required to pay for rice, chickens, and other produce acquired in the *barrios*. Confidence of tenant farmers was won by assigning young lawyers in uniform to fight their cases against landowners in the courts; one result was increased intelligence on Huk movements. Insurgents who were reluctant to surrender for fear of reprisals when they returned home were won over by promises of land and a new life on the frontier in Mindanao. There was a deliberate effort to school army officers to acquire a "social conscience" and see themselves as defenders of the constitution; given such leadership and support, Filipino officers and men, most of whom came from humble origins, soon rose to the national challenge.

This military effort was matched by renewed attention to healthier economic development. After liberation the U. S. had helped re-establish the Bureaus of Public Health, Fisheries, Highways, Weather and other specialized services. Late in 1950 the Philippine and U. S. governments signed the Quirino-Foster Agreement pledging joint support to a development program giving substance to recommendations of the American "Bell Mission" that earlier had surveyed needs in the Islands. The U. S. imposed conditions for this aid, withholding actual grants until the Phil-

83

ippine Congress had signified its general agreement and enacted tax measures insuring availability of funds to meet governmental operating expenses and a minimum wage law. In the mid-spring of 1951 a U. S. Economic Cooperation Administration Mission to the Philippines was established. Initially, its assigned task was one of economic and social development plus technical assistance. During the first several years the Mission encouraged reforms such as enactment by the Philippine Congress of a "Magna Charta of Labor," setting aside compulsory arbitration of disputes and establishing free collective bargaining. However, with the passage of time and consolidation of bureaucratic procedures this Mission lost sight of these broader objectives of social reform; it has focused primarily upon technical innovations within Philippine Government bureaus and some assistance to industry, lending little help to Filipinos struggling with more fundamental problems.

A reawakening of Filipinos to their political heritage was crucial in helping the Republic survive. A vigorous and free press centering on Manila and rapidly multiplying radio stations in the capital and the provinces are among the vital institutions of the land. In this national emergency Filipino newspapermen often performed courageously, exposing abuses of official power and arousing the people. Civic organizations, including the Lions, Rotary, Junior Chamber of Commerce, Catholic Action, the Young Men's Christian Association and the League of Women Voters, now provided forums where public problems were discussed and opposition leaders could be heard. As the 1951 elections approached, a National Movement for Free Elections was formed to safeguard the polls. The Army and the Constabulary, newly aware of their national responsibility, were employed to insure a free and peaceful election—with near complete success—and the opposition Nacionalista Party afforded an opportunity to capture control of the Senate. The opposition also won handily in Manila, electing as Mayor, Arsenio Lacson, a former newspaper columnist, boxer, and congressman who proceeded with a well-publicized house cleaning at City Hall.

As public confidence in elected government was gradually restored, the campaign against the Huk rebellion proceeded with new vigor. At its peak the Communist-led revolt had relied upon the armed strength of some 10,000 insurgents supported by another 30,000 irregulars. A succession of Huk military defeats in the field, loss of support as farmers learned to trust the government, and the arrest of most Politburo members, broke the rebellion as a major movement. The remaining Huks split into bands that lived furtively in the mountains and supported themselves by banditry. Although the struggle against these groups was to continue for many years, the armed challenge to governmental authority on Luzon had been overcome.

The popular movement for reform gathered momentum and national demand for a new type of leadership began to make itself felt. Almost inevitably attention centered upon Ramón Magsaysay, who had captured the imagination of Filipinos with his successful defeat of the Huks, combined with concern for justice and attention to the "felt needs" of the ordinary *tao* or farmer. One evening in November, 1952, Magsaysay was invited to the home of Senator Tañada for a secret conference with veteran Nacionalista Party Chairman Eulogio Rodriguez, Senator José Laurel and Senator Claro Recto. These senior opposition leaders were in search of a candidate for their party; they had determined that the youthful Secretary of Defense—he was then forty-five years old—possessed both the appeal that would capture votes and the following within the military that would insure the Army fulfilling its new role as guardian of the electoral process. The highly personalized character of Philippine politics with its emphasis upon individual and family association rather than party allegiance made such a switch acceptable. In keeping with the agreement signed and locked away that evening Magsaysay agreed to become the Nacionalista candidate and if elected president to seek the advice of the Party leaders in making appointments. Magsaysay resigned as

86

Secretary of Defense early in 1953 and was nominated by a neatly managed Nacionalista convention. Opposition forces were further strengthened when the incumbent Liberal Party split over Quirino's insistence upon campaigning for re-election despite his ill health. The resulting new Democratic Party containing substantial elements of the "sugar bloc" made an abortive attempt to support Carlos P. Romulo for president; when this enterprise floundered, independent-minded leaders of this movement such as Senator Tomás Cabili led their faction in supporting Magsaysay, accepting in return Nacionalista support for their Congressional candidates.

The electoral campaign of 1953 differed radically from all earlier political contests in the Islands. Formerly, candidates had been content to rely upon the pledged support of provincial political leaders who through their economic dominance, kinship ties and old allegiances marshalled their followers. Now, the opposition forces with Magsaysay as their symbol created the first mass political movement in Philippine history and ordinary citizens joined in the contest as never before. They aimed to overcome the immense advantage enjoyed by the administration; the president was empowered to suspend governors and mayors and shift appointed personnel. The Magsaysay-For-President movement gathered the talents of veterans, ex-guerrillas, idealistically motivated younger Fili-

87

pinos, and many others into a national organization that claimed a million members. Women also joined and helped in house-to-house canvassing to check voter registration. While Quirino was largely immobilized by illness and had to rely upon campaigning by his running mate, former House Speaker José Yulo, Magsaysay and his fellow candidates moved into the *barrios*, shaking hands, listening to the problems of ordinary folk and promising remedies. On election day school teachers serving as chairmen and poll clerks on precinct boards of electoral inspectors supervised the voting; they acted under national direction by the Commission on Elections, which insured a determined impartiality. Returns when tallied showed that Magsaysay had been elected by roughly a two-to-one majority of some 5,000,000 votes cast. For the first time the Republic had managed an orderly and popular transfer of power from one political party to another, setting a consequential precedent in these formative years.

Inauguration of Ramón Magsaysay and his vice-presidential running mate, Carlos P. Garcia, on December 30, 1953, raised Filipino expectations of government concern for popular welfare to heights it is doubtful that any administration could have fulfilled. Despite the energy of its leaders and their dedication to a new order of national emphasis, the administration was handicapped from the outset; it lacked both

88

an experienced "brain trust" and clearly formulated and tested ideas for national action on the most stubborn social and economic problems confronting the Philippines. Guided by the instincts of its leaders and the promises made during the campaign, Magsaysay's administration focused its attention upon difficulties that in time often proved symptomatic of deeper problems. In keeping with this spirit he opened Malacañang Palace to all who wanted to bring him their troubles. Magsaysay established a Presidential Complaints and Action Commission, under Manuel Manahan, a former publisher who was one of the President's more dedicated supporters. Citizens throughout the Islands were invited to send letters and telegrams of complaint direct to the President; the Commission investigated these, acted to redress wrongs and compelled a new respect for performance among officialdom.

A Court of Agrarian Relations was established to speed action on cases of tenant farmers and assure them of equality before the law. To help meet rural needs the administration created an Agricultural Tenancy Commission and the Agricultural Credit and Cooperative Financing Agency. There was energetic attention to drilling wells in the *barrios* to provide potable drinking water and constructing pre-fabricated school houses. Through the National Resettlement and Rehabilitation Administration the government tried to move landless families to the frontier in Mindanao and Palawan and provide them with their own farms. The first step toward self-government in the *barrios* was taken with enactment of a law that enabled villages to elect their own councils to replace the officials formerly appointed by the municipal mayors. With official encouragement the labor movement prospered; both the number of unions and total membership roughly doubled.

Each period of accelerated national enterprise seems to be followed by a relapse toward the old patterns of activity, until the society again can muster the energy for a renewed attack upon its problems. By the time Magsaysay, Cabili and all their fellow passengers except one were killed in a midnight plane accident on Cebu in March, 1957, the first enthusiasm commanding widespread national support for rapid change had spent itself. With the loss of its most dynamic leader, the Philippine Republic shifted toward the former methods of managing official business; government largely ceased to be the means for innovation and the older generation of political leaders reasserted themselves. President Carlos P. Garcia sought to continue some programs launched by his predecessor and give new attention to industrialization. By experience and instinct, however, he was inclined to wait for popular initiative to express itself while according high respect for the legal process. He did support the granting of steadily greater autonomy to chartered cities.

Thereby citizens were given an opportunity to decide more of their problems at home rather than needing always to seek help from Malacañang. This encouraged the development of new centers of local political power where younger men and women could prove themselves as independent public administrators. However, the Republic now paid the price for the failure to develop centers for "research in depth" on its economic and human problems from which could come sound guides to national effort.

The presidential elections of November, 1957, saw the return to office of President Garcia and most of his supporters; the opposition Liberal Party was unable to generate a mass response to its candidate, José Yulo, although a Liberal Vice-President, Diosdado Macapagal, was elected. With Manuel Manahan as their candidate, most of the younger followers of Magsaysay had left the administration and formed a third party, the Progressives, that sought support as the "true" heirs of their late leader. But they were unable to overcome the organized power of the two older parties and suffered also from lack of their own inspectors at the polls. During the 1959 elections this group joined with other leaders who had broken away from the two major parties and formed the Grand Alliance, which proved no more successful at establishing a political "third force." These experiences encouraged some of the abler young leaders, including

Raul Manglapus, Manuel Manahan, Francisco Rodrigo, and Emmanuel Pelaez—who had sponsored the "Barrio Charter" in Congress that strengthened self-rule in the villages—and many of their colleagues to join the opposition Liberals; they reasoned that the Philippines is wedded to the two-party system and that most could be accomplished within this established framework.

From these beginnings emerged the United Opposition of the Liberal Party that in the presidential election of 1961 brought a new dispensation to Philippine political life. For four years Vice President Macapagal and his associates quietly had toured the *barrios,* traveling to the most remote Islands and expounding their views on the rights of Filipinos and the need for new leadership. Through the hectic months of summer and autumn the Republic experienced the exhilaration, confusion, and cost of these quadrennial electoral contests. The incumbent Nacionalistas were favored to win, in the opinion of most professional politicians and observers; President Garcia who led their ticket was limited by the constitution to serving a total of eight years, insuring the occupancy of Malacañang during the final months of the next term by whoever was elected vice president. This prospect encouraged three contenders for the post; Senator Gil Puyat who campaigned on the Nacionalista ticket, Sergio Osmeña, Jr. who ran as an independent and the Liberal candidate, Emmanuel Pelaez.

The Nacionalistas controlled the administration, with its considerable patronage, the majorities in Congress and three-fourths of the governorships. They also were supported by large financial interests beholden to the government for exchange allocations, credits and other advantages. But despite these odds, victory in the elections held on November 14th went to the Liberals. Diosdado Macapagal at the age of fifty was chosen the fifth president of the Republic and Emmanuel Pelaez elected as Vice President. The Liberals also won six of the eight contested seats for the Senate; in the House of Representatives the Nacionalistas returned to control. Not only had the Republic managed its second peaceful transfer of power from one political party to another, but the Filipino people had shown that they could be independent-minded in their choice of leaders, regardless of all efforts exerted to persuade them otherwise.

The tasks confronting the new administration of President Macapagal are such as to challenge even the most courageous and idealistic of its members. For the Philippine Republic to date has fallen short of meeting the expectations of most of its citizens. It has surmounted the first critical years of independence, demonstrating greater stability, regard for individual freedom and mastery of democratic meth-

93

ods than most new nations. This in itself is a major achievement, considering the handicaps with which Filipinos embarked upon this enterprise following the close of World War II. Due primarily to maintenance of integrity in the electoral process, Filipinos do accept the ballot box as their instrument for change and this has reaffirmed faith in their essential political institutions. The great concern now of the 28,000,000 citizens of the Republic is to make theirs a productive nation that also affords social and economic democracy and is prepared to cope with the external world in which it must make its way. Filipinos feel the eyes of their Asian neighbors are upon them, and are aware that because of their Christian and political heritage from the West their role in these troubled times has wide significance.

# 5. The Economy

Economic life in this varied and naturally rich Archipelago is viewed from many perspectives. A Filipino engineer or government administrator wrestling with improvement of roads and extension of hydroelectric power systems sees it as a developing economy needing ever more energy and better communications. One of Manila's younger "robber barons" who is floating a new stock company may view the present as an opportunity to create a financial empire and sometimes capitalizes upon nationalism to further his aims. An American prospector who arrived with the army and stayed to marry and make his home is convinced the Philippines is a land of extraordinary mineral wealth, betrayed by outcrops of ore in often little explored and hardly accessible mountainous hinterlands. In the provinces a Chinese retail store operator thinks the Islands offer an advantageous place to do business; competition is less keen than it was in his ancestor's homeland, his use of the abacus affords a distinct advantage in calculating most business transactions and customers are readily bound by extending them credit. But the estimate that matters most is that of Juan de la Cruz, or Mr. Average Citizen, and his family. Their first concern is with employment opportunity and the availability at prices they can afford of the essentials for daily living; their budget is primarily devoted to fish, rice, corn, coconuts, vegetables, tropical fruits, *bagoong*—a paste of fermented shrimp or fish prized for seasoning—textiles, a few luxuries such as cigars or cigarettes, soft and hard drinks and cosmetics for the younger ladies.

Despite new and energetic attention to building factories and expanding service industries, more than two out of every three Filipinos still depend for their livelihood upon farming and fishing. To appreciate both their present circumstances of life and the prospects for improving them we must look carefully at the agricultural pursuits. Today some 75 percent of the export earnings of the Republic are derived from farm crops. Likewise, food imports are prominent among the items that absorb the ever-scarce foreign exchange. Yet, it is estimated that two to three times the area now cultivated could be soundly planted to annual and perennial crops, provided the new skills of soil conservation are effectively employed. Experiments also indicate that application of modern scientific techniques to fields now under cultivation could double and sometimes quadruple the crop harvest. The Islands hold the promise that development of these resources can afford a richer and more varied way of life for Filipinos and simultaneously contribute substantially to food and resource needs in more crowded neighboring Asian lands.

Some 160,000,000 coconut trees, growing chiefly within sight of the sea on the numerous islands, provide a living for one out of every four Filipinos. Approximately 7,000,000,000 nuts harvested annually make the Philippines the world's largest grower: during the past six years about one-half of all coconut products moving in international trade came from these Islands, earning the Republic roughly $150,000,000 (U. S.) annually. These exports are primarily in the form of copra—the dried white meat of the coconut—and of coconut oil that has been expressed by mills from this meat. A principal market is in Northern Europe, where the oil is used in manufacturing and where Dutch and Danish farmers feed the residual copra meal to their dairy cattle. The other major market is in the United States, where coconut oil long has been important for the soap and other industries. The Philippines also is one of the largest exporters of desiccated coconut, the shredded meat of the fresh nut that is mechanically dried and is prized by candy makers and housewives abroad. Although they do not enter into the trade statistics, many coconuts also are consumed by Filipinos at home. They are a favorite source of cooking oil and shortening. The tender meat of the young coconut is a constituent in many Filipino dishes. In some regions the flower stalks are tapped for their juice, which ferments to make *tuba,* the most popular of light alcoholic rural drinks.

Although coconuts are found growing in almost every part of the Philippine Islands, a few regions specialize in commercial production. The most important area is in eastern and southern Luzon—Quezon Province alone has some 36,000,000 coconut trees. Other principal coconut growing areas are in Leyte, Samar, and eastern Negros and around the northern, western and southern fringes of Mindanao. Coconuts occupy nearly 3,000,000 acres of land. Particularly in Mindanao they can be found growing on large plantations of up to 2,500 acres. But a substantial proportion of production also comes from small farmsteads whose owners depend upon 50 or 100 trees to provide a small cash income to supplement their subsistence crops. The annual yield of nuts per tree varies greatly; in some of the less fertile areas of Luzon a harvest of 40 nuts is common, while the more productive plantations in Zamboanga may produce nearly 100 nuts per tree.

Coconuts traditionally are thought of as the lazy farmer's crop; once the trees begin to bear at the age of about seven years nuts are gathered three or four times annually, the outer husk is removed, the nuts cracked and the white meat lifted out to dry in the sun or in a mechanical drier. Copra buyers—often Chinese—collect the sacks of dried coconut meat from the barrios and deliver them to an oil mill or assemble them for export at a pier where foreign ships can dock. Plants manufacturing desiccated coconut depend upon a daily supply of fresh nuts picked up by trucks from the growers. Scientists, however, have found that this traditional system of farming can be modified, vastly increasing the yield of nuts. Leguminous cover crops and fertilizer can speed the bearing of trees and often enhance harvests by 50 percent. Methods have been tested for reducing damage by rats that like to nest in the coconut crowns and by beetles attacking the flowers. Despite extended research work scientists have yet to discover a solution to the dreaded *cadang cadang* disease that has destroyed some 9,000,000 trees in the Bicol Peninsula over the past thirty years. But trees resistant to the disease have been found. Although there has been little breeding of superior strains, a few growers raise coconut trees that bear in three or four years and offer promise for planting large idle areas to this producer of valuable oils.

During recent years the Philippines has supplied roughly one spoonful out of every ten in the American sugar bowl; with the curtailment of U. S. imports from Cuba the permanent quota admitting 952,000 tons of sugar annually is being augmented, at least temporarily, by some 50 percent. This development indicates the potential of this second largest export industry in the Islands. Although founded during the Spanish era, the modern sugar industry was fostered with official support and financing by the Insular Government during and following World War I. By the early 1930's the Philippines had become a major world supplier, producing about 1,500,000 tons of sugar from 500,000 acres of land. Fear of this competition prompted pressure upon the U. S. Congress, which in 1934 established the quota system controlling sales in the American market, and limited imports from the Islands to roughly two-thirds of their output. From that date until very recently the industry made scant growth, relying for expansion upon modest increases in domestic consumption, which now totals about 400,000 tons annually. This static character of the industry discouraged modernization in many mills and plantations and contributed to grave social problems in some sugar growing areas, as poorly paid plantation laborers increased in numbers and competed for the limited employment opportunities. It also fostered a tendency among many planters to seek advantage by mustering political support rather than by improving their technical efficiency.

The greatest sugar growing region in the Philippines is on the Island of Negros, where rich soils, a near absence of typhoons, and comparatively favorable rainfall permit the highest yields. Central Luzon ranks next in importance as a sugar cane growing region, followed by Panay, Cebu and Mindoro. Unlike Hawaii and some other sugar producing regions where a mill and surrounding cane-growing land is owned and operated by one company, the industry in the Philippines is a cooperative venture. The 25 sugar *centrals* that grind the cane and produce centrifugal sugar are supplied, usually over private railways, with cane from some 100,000 sugar farms owned by families or individuals. These plantations are worked by hired laborers that either live on the *hacienda* or are brought in for work chiefly at the cutting season. An estimated 3,000,000 Filipinos depend upon the sugar industry for a livelihood, either directly or indirectly. The industry, which earns the Philippines about $120,000,000 or more annually in foreign exchange, forms the largest single commercial investment in the Islands—total capital involved is reported as equivalent to $800,000,000. Major shipping, banking, insurance, equipment supply, and fertilizer marketing organizations depend upon this modern complex of sugar production.

There is another, much smaller, and yet significant sugar industry whose production does not enter into the national statistics—this is the home industry producing the dark brown *muscavado* for local consumption and sometimes export. Smaller farmers engaged in this enterprise grow their cane on plots where they crush out the juice in crude mills, often powered by a *carabao* walking in circles. The residual *bagasse* is burned to evaporate the juice. When the dark liquid begins to crystalize it is cooled, crushed, and bagged for sale in *sarisari* (small rural variety stores). In some areas the liquor is hardened in half of a coconut shell and provides a common staple for local trade. Rural entrepreneurs also occasionally convert the cane juice into a highly potent alcoholic drink.

While the sugar industry has begun to explore chemurgy and pulp manufacture from *bagasse,* growing of cane still offers substantial possibilities for modernization. Postwar rehabilitation permitted a consolidation of sugar mills into larger and more efficient units—although there are about one-half as many *centrals* today as prewar they have an equal capacity. With the introduction of pump irrigation and increased use of chemical fertilizer a substantially smaller acreage now produces an annual output equal to that of the early 1930's. While the industrial workers in the *centrals* have benefited from recent national concern with enforcement of the minimum wage law, unionization, housing, medical care and social security, few of these advantages have been extended to the plantation laborers. Their wages are increasing, but most continue to be paid less than the equivalent of $1 per day. More serious is the underemployment. Diversification of crops and raising of livestock offer a partial solution on many plantations. But the future of Filipinos in the industry depends chiefly upon improving methods to lower production costs in order to compete, and upon markets abroad for sugar, of which the Philippines could supply substantially greater tonnages.

While coconut products and sugar provide the chief export earnings for the Islands, three other crops are also of importance—abaca, tobacco and pineapples. Under the trade name of Manila hemp, abaca from the Philippines supplies perhaps 90 percent of the world market for this fiber that is used for rope, twine, and some types of carpeting. Competition from metallic and synthetic fibers during recent years and invasion of abaca growing farms by mosaic disease has made this a declining industry that today provides about 8 percent of export earnings. By contrast, growing of tobacco has expanded to about 200,000 acres.

Introduction of Virginia-type tobacco to meet the domestic demand for cigarette manufacture now is supplanting former production of darker tobacco used in the popular Manila cigars. During recent years exports of tobacco leaf, stems and scraps sometimes have exceeded 10,000 tons; the chief market is Spain, although other European countries and the United States are included among the buyers. Pineapples are raised throughout the Islands as a household fruit and sold in local markets. Commercial growing and canning are done chiefly at Del Monte on the cool Bukidnon Plateau in northern Mindanao. Here on a plantation covering 17,000 acres is produced a substantial portion of the pineapple served on American tables—exports fluctuate from 21,000 tons to 78,000 tons annually.

Among food crops grown for domestic consumption rice is by far the most important—Filipino families in the cities calculate the cost of living according to the price of one *ganta,* a cubic measure holding about 4.5 pounds of milled rice. Many insist that wages should be linked to the cost of this basic commodity. Actually, over 1,000 different varieties of rice are grown in the Islands, including the prized gleaming white *wagwag* and such unusual strains as the naturally herb scented *camenan* from Iloilo. Annual harvests in recent years have been in the neighborhood of 2,300,000 tons of milled rice; this is barely adequate for consumption

needs and imports regularly are authorized to stabi-
lize prices of this staple that is eaten by three out of
every four Filipinos.

Although it occupies such a crucial role in the economy of Filipino families, rice growing in the Islands
remains much underdeveloped. An estimated 70 percent of production is from lowland varieties cultivated
in the traditional Asian pattern. Diked fields are
flooded, usually at the beginning of the rainy season.
The soil then is worked into a muddy consistency,
usually with a carabao-drawn wooden plow, although
mechanical preparation with tractors is beginning.
After the clods are broken and levelled with a simple
harrow, fifteen-inch high rice seedlings from the nursery plots are transplanted into the fields by hand,
with the women joining in this community enterprise
when families help each other. Rice fields are weeded
less carefully in the Philippines than in Formosa and
Japan and only a few farmers have begun to use
chemical fertilizer and insecticides to control pests.
When nearly ripe the grain stalks are cut by hand and
the sheaves gathered. A few of the larger farms use
powered threshing equipment. But the traditional
method is to beat off the heads of grain over the lip
of a large basket or on a bamboo platform and hand
winnow grain in the wind. In populous regions me-
chanically powered rice mills hull and polish the grain.
But in the hinterland "hand-pounding" still is com-

mon; grain is placed in a large wooden pestle and beaten with the end of a wooden mortar. Although this system is more primitive it leaves on the grain a portion of the red bran that is rich in vitamins and protein—doctors observe that beriberi is less common in communities not served by modern rice mills. Upland rice which accounts for about 30 percent of Philippine production is harvested and threshed in much the same manner. Instead of relying upon irrigation and dikes, however, these sloping fields are plowed, or simply burned if they are part of a new clearing in the forest. Rice seed is broadcast and covered with use of a *carabao* harrow. Both in the lowlands and uplands storage facilities often are primitive; most containers are large woven baskets affording little protection against rats and insects. A significant portion of the crop so laboriously gathered is lost for human consumption.

These traditional methods of rice growing offer great opportunities for expanding yields; improved methods are beginning to be applied, particularly on the larger *haciendas* in the "rice basket" of the central Luzon Plain and around the shores of Laguna de Bay, southeast of Manila. Farmers there are finding that dependable year-round irrigation often enables them to double the harvest per crop and grow two crops annually instead of one. The soil surveys needed to insure effective use of chemical fertilizer still are fragmentary and some farmers complain that increased fertilization attracts many more pests. Scientifically managed plots have produced two to three times the yield of even the better rice fields, but a great need exists for breeding of more productive and disease resistant varieties of rice seed. The average Filipino farmer also is handicapped for lack of a good farm wagon to move lime and fertilizer onto his fields and transport the harvest to market; most depend today upon a *carabao* sled that carries about 300 pounds.

Application of modern, tested methods for expanding rice production is hindered, however, by a largely archaic land tenure system. The owner-operating farmer in the Philippines is a rarity. Instead, rice fields commonly are owned by families who have acquired them through inheritance or purchase and worked by tenants on a share basis. This is true both of large *haciendas* that may cover a thousand acres or more and the numerous small holdings of as little as two or three acres. Traditionally, in most provinces tenants receive one-half of the crop in return for working the land. Although the Rice-Share Tenancy Act now legally assures the tenant of 70 percent of the harvest when he supplies his own work animals and seed, this law is not always enforced. Many tenants remain obligated to the landowners through indebtedness and lack the capital to invest in modern methods. Most land owners who often have moved to the cities and are occupied with other pursuits give scant attention to applying improved practices on their holdings. Despite these obstacles ideas for improving production are filtering into the *barrios*. The effectiveness with which they are applied will depend substantially upon the success of the Court of Agrarian Relations and private groups in establishing a new and more secure incentive for operating farmers and upon the ability of rural Filipinos to overcome "social inhibitions" that are the product of ignorance and familial obligations.

Corn, which the Spanish priests introduced from Mexico, has become the second most important staple in the diet of Filipinos; it is favored particularly by residents of the Central Visayan Islands, by settlers on the frontiers in the Cagayan Valley of Northeastern Luzon, in Mindanao, and as a dry season crop in some rice-growing areas. The flint type corn that Filipinos prefer is cracked and polished, either by hand or machine, to remove the bran. It is then cooked and eaten as the principal starch component of the meal. Since corn is cheaper than rice and its consumption connotes less social prestige, it frequently is blended with rice in communities where the latter is scarce or expensive, although traditionally corn-eating people in the Islands are judged to be more vigorous than those who depend entirely upon rice. In season corn also is eaten green as a favored vegetable and even is cooked in the husk and sold hot on the streets of Manila and other cities.

Corn is grown chiefly as an upland crop, one that unfortunately encourages severe erosion on steep hillsides, and annual production now approximates 1,000,000 tons of shelled corn. And new markets are developing for corn as it becomes accepted as an ingredient in modern poultry feeds and livestock supplements. Although improvement in corn yields is not so hampered by the tenancy system that inhibits application of better methods for growing rice—most corn is grown by small owner-cultivators—average yields are miserably low when compared to proven possibilities. The subsistence farmer who clears and plows an upland plot of leached-out land and plants his native unselected seed that produces a few scrawny ears often harvests only 250 to 400 pounds of shelled corn per acre. Yet a few more progressive farmers, including young Four-H Club members, are achieving crop yields well over twelve times as high by planting new hybrid varieties, fertilizing properly, and applying other improved practices. Indications are that the Philippines could duplicate the great revolution in corn growing which brought vast expansion of yields in Iowa, Illinois and elsewhere in the American Middle West during the past three decades. And in many areas of the Islands it is possible to grow two and even three crops of corn annually.

With rare exceptions Filipino families eat a high-starch diet; native staple grains plus imported wheat and flour are supplemented with numerous root crops that are boiled and served plain or mixed with vegetables, meat, or sea food. Approximately 1,400,000 tons (moist weight) of these tubers now are grown yearly. Most important among these is the sweet potato or *camote* that is a favorite crop among upland farmers. Another is the tapioca plant known in its native Latin American home as *mandiocca,* that also yields a starch with industrial uses in making alcohol, paper, and glue. The taro root of the South Pacific, known in the Islands as *gabi,* provides a common substitute for rice. Commercial production of the Irish potato now is beginning to make this a common item of diet, particularly in the cities. Although Westerners think of them as a fruit, Filipinos frequently cook bananas as a vegetable; dozens of varieties are found in the Islands including the short, fat *saba* that must be boiled or fried before it is eaten, the tiny delicious "finger of the virgin," and other succulent fruits that are yellow, red or green when ripe. So far there has been scant attention to selection and development of improved varieties, though the banana promises one of the highest yields per land unit of any crop grown in the moist Asian tropics and could become a major source of food for growing populations in the region.

The world of tropical fruits and vegetables so far

has commanded comparatively little attention from scientists, although it holds promise of great and sometimes delicious abundance. Philippine mangoes are among the tastiest grown anywhere and are now finding favor abroad. The delicately flavored mangosteen, the tart *lanzones,* the crunchy-fleshed chico or sapodilla forming the fruit of the tree that also yields chicle for chewing gum, milky-juiced star apples and the giant jack fruit all are regularly found in markets. The rambutan, relative of the Chinese and Indian lichi, and the giant santol from Bangkok are new favorites with orchardists as are many varieties of citrus. Avocado, which Filipinos usually eat with cream and sugar, are so common in some regions of the Islands that they are fed to pigs in season. While temperate vegetables including carrots, onions, cabbage, beets, celery, watermelons, and muskmelons are becoming plentiful, some of the greatest opportunities for enriching the diet are in the native vegetables; high-protein *sigadilla* and *malungai,* mungo beans, peanuts and some of their botanical relatives can be grown with comparative ease but are inadequately appreciated nutritionally. Although they are beginning to be raised as a commercial crop, cacao and several varieties of coffee, including the flavorful *arabica,* usually are grown by Filipinos as a backyard plant for home use. The infant development of domestic seed and nursery firms offering tested planting material for sale and the difficulty of distribution throughout the Islands, however, have inhibited Filipinos from taking full advantage of the wealth in nourishment and flavor their gardens might produce.

While the *carabao* remains the most important animal in the Filipino farmer's scheme of life, there is new and energetic attention to improving many other types of livestock. Hybrid hogs far superior to the razor-backed native types now are becoming popular with farmers, who often sell their pigs when small to be roasted whole over a fire and served as the *lechon* desired for festive occasions. Imported milk goats are being crossed with the hardy native strains that now are chiefly raised for meat. A few successful herds of dairy cows have been started and there is increasing attention to milking the *carabao* and cross-breeding this draft animal with the higher yielding Indian Murrah buffalo. But the Philippines continues to import some $10,000,000 worth of dairy products annually. The local beef industry is beginning to recover from wartime devastation of breeding stock, although meat imports remain important. Horses rarely are used in the fields. Instead, most are employed for riding or pulling the two-wheeled *calesas* used in many provincial cities for public transport. Modern poultry farming is a rapidly expanding industry, providing eggs and broilers for the growing cities. Ducks are raised less for meat than for their eggs, which are incubated until nearly ready to hatch, when they are sold, particularly in Tagalog regions, as *balut* to be cooked with a pinch of salt and eaten hot between meals as a snack—doctors often recommend this for patients needing special nourishment.

Fish and rice mean to Filipinos much the same as do meat and potatoes to families in Europe and America. Despite the national taste for sea foods and their relative abundance in seas surrounding the Islands, the Philippines continues to import fish in many forms. The annual value of importations of fish approximates $9,000,000, ranking next in importance among food importations after wheat and other cereals and dairy products. While inshore fishing with small craft and simple gear is a part- or full-time occupation for a great many Filipinos, there has been little development of large scale catching from the ocean. Capital and technical knowledge for such operations is largely lacking and much scientific investigation remains to be done in locating fishing grounds in nearby waters. By contrast Filipinos have developed to a fine art the raising of fish in ponds with controlled water supply and artificial fertilization. Among the many types of marine life marketed from these ponds the *bangus* or milkfish is a particular delicacy. It accounts for a substantial portion of the approximately 442,000 tons of fresh fish consumed annually. The slow increase in cultured and caught fish, however, lags behind the rate of national population growth and a frequently voiced hope of Filipino housewives is for a cheap and abundant supply of sea food; inhabitants of fishing villages, while often poor, betray their higher protein diets with sturdier physiques than most of their countrymen.

Within recent years exploitation of the fine stands of tropical hardwoods scattered throughout the Islands has grown rapidly to become a major industry—forest products now rank third in importance as a source of foreign exchange, earning the Republic more than $90,000,000 annually and accounting for some 14 percent of the national income. These timber stands remained largely untouched by commercial exploitation throughout the centuries of Spanish rule. Even during the first years of the American era the Philippines was a net importer of lumber. Now this pattern has been reversed and Philippine Mahogany is finding increasing favor with builders in Europe and America. Originally, the industry relied upon small sawmills that supplied the local market and a few larger mills manufacturing for export. Within the past decade numerous plywood plants relying primarily upon Philippine exports of logs have been established in Japan and several in Formosa, Korea and elsewhere in the Far East—there are also a few plants in the United States that import logs or veneer to surface their plywood. More recently plywood factories have been erected in the Islands and Filipinos are beginning to process their forest products at home, producing plywood for domestic use and foreign sale.

The Philippine timber industry has the potential of becoming a permanent, major national source of income and employment comparable to that of Finland and several other countries. This will require thorough application of conservation practices that today are honored more in name than in fact. Many logging enterprises, particularly among the smaller companies, operate today on the philosophy of "cut and get out." Concern with immediate returns and lack of regard for the needs of the next generation of Filipinos result from more than a desire for profits; there is relentless pressure by farmers to move in upon newly logged forests and reap the bounty of rich virgin soils. This is aggravated by the problem of the *caingineros,* who cut and burn the forest, plant a few crops of corn or upland rice and move to another site when fertility declines and weeds take over. For many centuries this was the means of livelihood of some aboriginal peoples in the more remote hinterland. Christian Filipinos, who traditionally inhabited the lowlands and practiced a permanent agriculture, adopted the system on a large scale during World War II when many retreated to the mountainous interior to escape the Japanese. Since independence, increasing population with its inevitable demand for new land has driven ever more Filipinos to seek such a subsistence livelihood in the forests; the process has been encouraged also by some powerful interests determined to expand their private holdings. Today this pattern of shifting agriculture is threatening the Republic's timber and water resources. Denuded slopes are giving way to erosion and floods that damage lowland farm areas and silt up the storage reservoirs for new hydro-electric installations.

Conservation and regeneration of the remaining forests require a far-sighted policy on the part of concession holders and stricter enforcement of government regulations in some areas. But the crucial problem is that of re-educating subsistence farmers in remote communities and it is they who have the least preparation for understanding modern agriculture. For many of them burning a new patch in the forest is a substitute for plowing, other land preparation with a *carabao* or tractor, and scientific use of green manure crops and chemical fertilizer. Experiments have shown that even upon infertile slopes corn yields can be multiplied five and six times only by interplanting perennial native legumes on the contour and annually cutting the green tops to provide mulch, water retention and nutrients. There is great promise also in replacing annual cultivated grain crops with permanent shrub and tree crops and improved pastures. But such a total planned approach to the ecology and human potential of a region has not yet been tried in

116

the Islands, although the problem is characteristic also of many other upland regions in the moist tropics.

The possibilities for greater utilization of Philippine forest resources are such as to excite the imagination of Filipino and foreign scientists who are pioneering in this field. Pulp and paper potentially can become great industries in the Islands; similar opportunities exist for the manufacture of the many types of building materials from wood chips and fibers. The basis for such development already exists in the waste left behind by most timber operators and in the less desirable trees that are now largely ignored. Experiments with growing bamboo and exotic species for use in making pulp and other products suggest that vast areas of idle grass land profitably could be planted to such permanent crops. Philippine tropical forests hold dozens of plants, such as the climbing rattan, that botanists feel have commercial possibilities; some are used for dyes, paints, and spices and others have medicinal properties. The growing of rubber trees has proven profitable in Southern and Western Mindanao and the Sulu Archipelago and a few plantations are producing, although natural and synthetic rubber still are imported. A crucial question for the future of the Republic is whether such permanent crops will be introduced in time to forestall major changes in the climate patterns of some Islands that would make them less hospitable to human habitation.

Although the Chinese had extracted minerals with crude methods in the Islands for centuries and the Spanish made repeated attempts to discover rich ore deposits, it remained for the Americans early in this century to organize mining as a major industry. When world prices for gold rose during the decade prior to World War II deposits in the Islands were exploited on a large scale, particularly in Mountain Province, the Bicol Peninsula and Northeastern Mindanao. Gold mining now has declined in importance as rising costs of operation had to be financed from a relatively fixed market price for the yellow metal. Instead, the postwar mining interest increasingly has shifted to exploitation of base metals. Mineral production, with an annual value exceeding $130,000,000, is becoming a vital industry, earning foreign exchange and producing the raw materials for domestic progress.

Discovery and development of new copper mines within recent years have made the Philippines the largest producer in the Far East. The first modern copper mines were opened at Mankayan in the mountains north of the summer capital of Baguio and on islands off the Bicol Peninsula. Large mines now also have been developed at Sipalay on the Southwestern coast of Negros, at Toledo on Cebu and on the island of Samar. Significant deposits are awaiting exploitation on Masbate, Northeastern Mindanao and several places on Luzon. Chromite deposits near Masinloc on the

Zambales coast continue to provide the largest single source of refractory ore in the Free World and chrome mining also is of importance. Production of manganese has been erratic, depending upon the output of small, rich deposits. Quicksilver is becoming a significant export and molybdenum is now being produced in limited quantities. Philippine iron ore is among the important exports to Japan and there is growing production of medium to low grade coal from the scattered deposits. Production of limestone for cement, rock asphalt, sand and gravel is also expanding with the construction industry.

With the principal exception of gold and silver, the pattern of Philippine mining has been one of producing ore or concentrates for export. Smelting and refining have been done abroad and sometimes the finished metal, as with copper, is returned to the Philippines for processing into wire, etc. Now copper smelting is being established as an industry and processing of other metals promises to follow. The future of the mining industry depends substantially upon the speed with which such technology is introduced. Deposits of yet untouched but proven ores are substantial and many others may remain to be discovered, but some of these largest known mineral resources can only be economically exploited with such advanced processing. Chief among these deposits is the huge nickel-iron laterite ore deposit in the Eastern Visayas and Northeastern

Mindanao, estimated at more than 1,000,000,000 tons. Such developments require cheap energy. Until present explorations determine whether the Islands do hold significant reserves of petroleum and natural gas, reliance must be placed upon expansion of hydroelectric power, and this demands substantial investment. Already the mining industry is fostering the skills and producing some of the raw materials that in time could stimulate creation of a significant chemical industry; one of the larger mining companies now is manufacturing chemical fertilizer as a by-product of its other operations.

The internal combustion engine is less of a mystery in the *barrios* of the Philippines than in the rural villages of any other country of Southeast Asia. This familiarity with machines is largely a heritage from the wartime liberation period, when the U. S. Army left tens of thousands of jeeps, trucks and other motor vehicles plus much heavy earth moving equipment throughout the Archipelago. Although often ignored by economists, this national mechanical awareness has been one of the factors contributing to the present "industrial surge" in the Islands; they are experiencing a rate of growth in manufacturing equalled in few other lands. The sounder large industries have been established to supply domestic markets which have expanded with the Republic's accelerated modernization. Others have been stimulated by shortages of products which during the past twelve years have been limited by exchange controls; these include some "packaging plants" that merely import goods in volume and place them in containers for sale. As these new industries have afforded opportunities for amassing wealth, dominant economic groups that once held most of their capital in rural and urban real estate have shifted a portion into manufacturing. The Philippines has begun to develop a distinct entrepreneurial class, a hierarchy of engineers and technicians, and a growing industrial labor force. A stock exchange that formerly offered primarily a market for mining shares now affords financing for public corporations engaged in processing and manufacturing. Mutual investment funds, insurance companies, government retirement and social security agencies and private individuals all are joining this venture in private enterprise.

A roster of consequential new industries suggests the extent to which the Philippines is developing a complex economy. Cement plants on Luzon and in the Visayas now provide for all domestic needs despite increasing demands of the construction industry and the highway paving program. They also supply new factories making cement blocks, tiles, soil pipe and numerous other products. A textile industry has mushroomed in recent years, relying chiefly upon imported raw cotton and synthetics. Local grown ramie is beginning to be processed at home with one factory spinning and weaving this durable fiber. Dozens of small shops and factories have been started, making shirts, *barong tagalogs* that Filipino men wear for dress occasions, ladies' garments, and industrial items such as sails, fishing nets and canvas. Two major oil refineries at Batangas and Mariveles on Bataan process imported crude oil into petroleum products. Most of the rubber tires rolling over Philippine highways are made locally, as are dozens of minor rubber products from tennis shoes to erasers. Assembly of automobiles from imported foreign components has become an important business for representatives of American and European car manufacturers. On the outskirts of Manila numerous shops, some with rudimentary assembly lines, convert surplus U. S. military jeeps into the colorful jeepneys that carry passengers over suburban and rural routes and the streets of the major metropolises. Milling of flour from imported wheat, pharmaceutical packaging, food canning, glass and paint manufacture, and assembly of radio and television receivers, air-conditioners, and numerous other consumer durables are representative of proliferating new enterprises that place the Philippines on the threshold of becoming an industrial nation.

Several key requirements for sustained and healthy progress in this industrial sector of the economy are still lacking, however. The government-managed National Power Corporation is expanding generation of hydroelectric power, particularly on Luzon and Mindanao. Where its transmission lines can be tapped and in the environs of Greater Manila, electric current is available at rates that encourage industrial consumption. But the great majority of the holders of private power franchises in the provinces charge such exorbitant rates for often undependable electric power as to discourage its commercial use. This also has inhibited rural electrification that otherwise might revolutionize life in the *barrios* where cheap power is needed for pump irrigation, rice mills, incubators and many other purposes. The Republic does not yet have a major basic steel industry, although several private and government establishments process steel products. Absence of substantial deposits of high grade coking coal means that the domestic exploitation of iron ore deposits, many of which are high in sulphur content, probably also will depend upon generating more inexpensive electric power. Promising sites do exist, particularly where the waters of Lake Lanao drop 2,000 feet to the sea near Iligan in north central Mindanao. In this geographically fragmented Archipelago competitive manufacturing and marketing only are possible with dependable and cheap inter-island transportation. At present, shipping rates between the Islands are so high and facilities so little developed as to hamper both the movement of bulk cargoes and perishables and creation of nation-wide retailing.

Despite a recent national annual rate of industrial expansion calculated by economists at 11 to 14 percent, the Republic still is troubled by unemployment. Government statistics show the unemployed number some 540,000 and another 506,000 are underemployed, working less than thirty hours each week; these figures are conservative and do not cover the labor force idle much of the year in rural areas. Tens of thousands of young college graduates are among those vainly searching for jobs. New service industries are absorbing a growing number, but many remain handicapped by a schooling emphasizing academic subjects and providing scant qualification for a role in manufacturing and modern agriculture. Expert mechanics are much in demand and command wages equivalent to $4 or $5 per day as contrasted to the minimum industrial wage of four *pesos* daily, or $1.35. Several critical skills, such as those of underground water geologists, are not available in the Islands. During the past decade foreign exchange controls have been so managed as to favor larger firms and individuals with political influence residing chiefly in and around Greater Manila. Ordinary Filipinos in the provinces have had little prospect of participating in international trade and frequently experience great difficulty in securing replacement parts for machines or imported seeds. With urbanization the emerging middle class and industrial labor group are beginning to offer a small market for mass produced goods. This prospect does not yet extend to most rural *barrios*, where annual cash income per family ordinarily is limited to a few hundred *pesos*, much of which must be devoted to paying debts and buying a few necessities. Yet experience is showing that given effective training, management, and opportunity, Filipinos can become fully competent in the skills demanded by modern industrial enterprise. A foreign construction firm that built one of the largest hydroelectric power dams in the Islands unexpectedly saved several million *pesos* because of the efficiency of Filipino laborers.

# 6. The Society, Its Religion, Arts and Pastimes

A Filipino boy or girl grows up and learns values in a unique family setting that strongly conditions all attitudes toward life; this childhood experience accounts for the strength of some institutions that buttress the Republic and for several of its most stubborn problems in bringing about progress. Changes in this pattern now beginning will determine how rapidly the Philippines can transform itself into a "modern" society with all this implies for development of its resources and people. Cultural anthropologists describe this as a centripedal or an extended family system. From infancy on, a young Filipino is not restricted to sharing the warmth of intimate affection with his or her parents, with the painful psychological stresses this frequently generates, as a child questions whether he or she is loved or is relegated to a less favored role. Rather, Filipino children find themselves part of a large yet intimately involved kinship group, where warm affection is shared with grandparents, god-parents, uncles, aunts, cousins, brothers and sisters and others. This kinship group is elaborated through-out life, most decisions regarding marriage, career, property, and even recreation being judged at least in part from this perspective.

While the Archipelago is a land of extraordinary variety, underlying patterns of motivation do hold for the 90 percent of the population that is Christian and extend to many of the pagan peoples. Children sleep in a common bed or in the same room with their parents and then with siblings to a much later age—even when housing space is ample—than is the practice in most Western societies; the fostering of early indi-vidual self-reliance rarely is prized as a goal. The contrast in childhood training given boys and girls accounts for some of the differences in their adult be-havior. From an early age girls are assigned house-hold responsibilities. They help with cooking, cleaning, baby-sitting and care of poultry, pigs and vegetables.

Among the non-Christians boys grow up thinking of themselves as hunters, travelers, talkers, and courters; there is little acceptance of sedentary careers demanding fixed and continuing routine work. Although the settled farm life of most Christians demands more sustained labor, early training is permissive and young males gladly shun such activities for more venturesome pursuits. The young Christian male does not match the finery of his pagan fellow-citizen who dresses more colorfully than the women of the community. But even the Manila urbanite prides himself on the exquisite weave of his *barong tagalog,* his manicured fingernails, his fancy watch and the polish on his shoes; the bearded man of the outdoors who glories in his rough and ready appearance would be a social outcast.

The Philippines still is largely a traditional society where the authority of the parental generation is strong, as is true throughout the Malayan world. The young regularly are reminded that the parents are responsible for their existence. Grandparents also are respectfully consulted, as are uncles and aunts. A young man frequently courts his mother-in-law-to-be as assiduously as the girl of his choice. This respect for the views of the older generation inhibits many a young Filipino from embarking upon a new type of career unfamiliar to his elders. Particularly in the provinces, the young Filipino rarely possesses significant cash or property until he is married. This reinforces the authority of the elders, as does the common practice of holding jointly inherited property. When children are left without parents or grandparents, the eldest, known in Tagalog as *panganay,* assumes responsibility including the right to punish; in rare circumstances personality may dictate that this role gravitate to another among siblings. But usually this one is late to marry, waiting for the others first to become settled. By contrast the youngest, known affectionately in Tagalog as *bunso,* is the pet of the family.

Christian Filipinos extend this familial pattern to include those not related by blood or marriage through a highly developed system of ritual kinship. Whenever there is to be a baptism, confirmation or marriage, godparents are selected for the occasion. While they are expected to insure religious instruction and support for the young should they lose their parents, the assumed responsibility extends far beyond this. A man who becomes a *compadre* or a lady who agrees to be a *comadre* henceforth is linked into the extended family, is expected to share festive occasions and exchange presents and becomes responsible also for the material welfare of this new set of relatives. This practice often is employed for political or financial advantage and an ambitious public figure may have many more godchildren than he can recognize. But the force of social pressure demands that he must help them when asked, even if it jeopardizes his career or his business. Likewise, when a Filipino establishes a firm new friendship, the tendency is to cement this through marriage to his sister or by making him a *compadre*.

Finding his principal emotional security within this extended family, the Filipino naturally inclines toward reinforcing the guarantees it affords. He seeks not so much independence for himself, but interdependence within a fold where relations to other members of the family are meticulously delineated in the respectful forms of address used even in casual conversation. By contrast, relations between non-kinsmen traditionally are delicate; though rarely mentioned, there usually is present in the background the implied question of what this association means for other members of the families concerned. As a consequence, business enterprises usually are built around a family and executives are chosen as much on the basis of blood or marriage relationship as on merit. A Filipino who has risen in the world helps his kin not only because he owes it to them, but also with the expectation that they later may help him. Because of the extent of this obligation Filipinos in the rural areas often tire of trying to "get ahead;" a farmer who has harvested an abundance of rice frequently finds that all of his born and adopted kinfolk expect to share it.

A Western scholar has described the Philippine Republic as an "anarchy of families." And the highly personalized character of politics underscores this. Senators and others may switch from one party to another and suffer few penalties. With many voters personal ties to leaders are more important than issues. An official's obligation to look after his family is used by him to sanction corruption. This preoccupation with advancing individual and family interests undoubtedly has inhibited appearance of a "proletarian consciousness" and growth of a significant class struggle—the tenant farmer aspires to becoming a landlord, and adopts this role when given an opportunity, rather than an independent owner-operating farmer associated with others of his kind. Repeated attempts to organize farmers' cooperatives have foundered upon this inclination to advance loans on the basis of relationship to the co-op manager rather than the prospects for productive use of the money and its probable repayment. With the exception of a few traditional pursuits including rice planting and harvesting and the *bayanihan*, when neighbors work together voluntarily in activities such as house-moving, it has been observed that Filipinos know how to live together wonderfully, but they rarely are able to cooperate effectively outside of the family. This individualistic and familial emphasis is evidenced in many ways. Fruit vendors compete alongside each other instead of joining in a common venture. Filipinos keep themselves and their homes immaculately clean while streets and public lavatories may be left cluttered with refuse. Yet,

131

this very fragmentation of the society has spared the Philippines much of the pain of many other new nations. Although it is a country composed of many distinctly different ethnic groups, Filipinos have not resorted to mass violence against each other as has happened on the South Asian sub-continent and elsewhere when one linguistic group fought another. While the Tagalog may make nasty remarks about the Pampangeño living across the river, his primary loyalty is not to any narrow ethnic nationalism but to his family. And in the process of emerging from this familial preoccupation, the Filipino is afforded an opportunity to cultivate a larger loyalty and consciousness.

The social upheaval fostered by World War II now is being accelerated by numerous influences including mass communications and is beginning to produce a society, particularly in the cities, wherein new motivations guide the Filipino. Rural women still are *seguristas* and want to own something safe. They usually manage the family purse. In the *barrios* men often tend toward the attitude of gamblers rather than calculating risk-takers; life, they feel, is pretty much a matter of luck, so why invest yourself and scant resources in something new and untried. The individual who finds his circumstance unbearable may run amok attacking others indiscriminately in a pattern of generalized hostility that affords an emotional rather than a rational solution. Most Filipino businessmen still

132

prefer to take over an established proven venture rather than pioneer a new one that might be more profitable. As in many formerly colonial areas, politics is the new arena where men prove themselves, as they once did in intra-community warfare and the hunt. Women remain the competent stabilizing force, managing the family store and much else. But in the army, in business, and in government service Filipinos are mastering new skills of management and decision-making that they now are applying to their developing economy and role in domestic and international activities. Young Filipinos—especially in the cities— are leaving secure jobs to take a chance on the frontier or in a burgeoning new business that may offer opportunity. Young couples are eloping more frequently and marrying mates of their own choice. In some families there is almost a "generational conflict" as the young challenge the decisions of their elders. The "inner directed" and also the "other directed" Filipino is beginning to be heard from as he seeks to give substance to the democratic ideal that a man can make his own fate provided he applies himself. There is a new interest in rational experimentation as contrasted to the traditional way of doing things that is beginning to feed ideas from the city back into the rural *barrios*.

The archetype of the Philippine society-to-be is not yet in evidence. And many questions are hostage to the future. In cultivating the more aggressive self-reliance that social mobility demands, will the Filipino sacrifice the warmth and psychological security the extended family now provides him? Will many Filipinas continue to accept the institution of *queridas,* or secondary wives, which is partly based on their assumption that men are after all irresponsible? Will the quest for advancement and the appetites generated by advertising in a cash economy lead parents to discipline and prod their sons in this new type of competitive effort? Where will the rural communities find leadership as the more creative younger people flock to the cities to join in this remaking of their society? Many Filipinos impatient to see their country modernized still are loath to sacrifice the kind of home life they now treasure. But they have yet to sort out a compromise that retains the most attractive features of the past while reaching for the new goals. Virtually no attention has been devoted to national designing of decentralized industrial development to minimize ills of urbanization and maximize prospects for retaining those features of family life that are among the boons Filipinos enjoy.

Most pervasive of all external influences molding these values within Philippine society is religion. Although religious practice often may be ritualistic, it still conditions the psychological environment in which even the impatient young Filipino intellectual must operate. This is true for the minorities who are Moslems and pagans as it is for the majority of Christians. It is revealing that almost every genuine mass movement in the Islands has had its religious dimension; even the Communist-led Huk guerrillas seeking recruits among the peasants of Central Luzon sought to use the teachings of Jesus Christ to justify their appeals for revolt. The Bible is their most fundamental literary work in the minds of many Filipinos and stories from the Scriptures are interwoven with folk tales. Over the past five years more than 1,200,000 copies of the Bible were distributed; most of these were printed in the eight major vernacular languages, but they also included English and Chinese versions.

Traditionally, religion largely reinforced the paternal character of Philippine society. It also inhibited acceptance of a more scientific and rational view of life that would encourage the Filipino to master his environment—revolutionary writers of the late nineteenth and early twentieth Centuries were scathing in their denunciations of the consequences for their people. This is today most apparent among the non-Christians. Ifugaos and other mountain peoples of Northern Luzon still regulate rice planting on their spectacular terraces with an eye to insuring that the spirits are favorably inclined, and the gods are relied upon to watch over the harvest. Despite all efforts

135

over the past half century to build a modern legal structure based upon Western precepts, the religious courts remain the most accepted authority among numerous tribes of Moslems in Mindanao and the Sulu Archipelago. The Hadji, who has fortified his status with a pilgrimage to Mecca, is respected to such a degree that he often expects to subsist without working. His efforts are devoted to teaching the Koran in Arabic, dispensing advice and mediating disputes.

Because of a chronic shortage of priests the Catholic Church during the Spanish era was more successful in introducing the forms of Christianity than in assuring a depth of comprehension of the faith among ordinary Filipinos. While this may have spared Filipinos the shattering of native institutions that characterized the Spanish conquest of the Incas, for example, it also meant that in folk practice Christianity was diluted with a vast body of nativistic belief. The almost blind faith of some individuals and sects in the healing afforded by religious rituals is one expression of this mixture; it is evident among those who flock to the Black Nazarene at Quiapo in Manila. Throughout the Islands numerous cases are reported of local citizens suddenly discovering miraculous intercession at the site of a particular cave or tree, although the Church repeatedly warns against such claims. Even in the modern period some farmers sought religious blessing of their rice seed before planting. Others in-

136

serted a small bamboo cross in the corner of their flooded paddy field to guard against worms attacking the crop. San Isidro de Labrador, the patron saint of agriculture in the Islands, was appealed to by farmers for relief from a crippling drought. Many farmers, hearing the teachings of the priests that it is easier for the poor to enter heaven, took this as a justification for not working to accumulate a reserve for the future.

It is one of the tragedies of this only predominantly Christian nation of the Orient that the alteration now under way in the role of religion in Filipino life has come not so much through more enlightened understanding of the Scriptures, but as a consequence of the impact of modern science, education, and technology. Instead of the Filipino building a total scheme of life around a new concept of his relationship to God, he often has tended to compartmentalize religion. Now mid-twentieth century influences are joining with aspirations for social mobility and security in the new world of industry, commerce, and urbanization to foster great religious changes. Some of these are taking place within the dominant Roman Catholic Church, that during recent decades has devoted much of its energy to education; in some communities these changes have cost the Church popularity, for poorer Filipinos found themselves unable to pay the tuition used to help finance the schools. Opportunities have developed, particularly since the war, for unorthodox Christian sects to gather converts. Like the Catholics, the Philippine Independent Church and the traditional Protestant groups are being challenged to evolve a quality of religious leadership that meets the felt needs of citizens in this rapidly emerging new nation.

To appreciate these influences that are shaping the inner character of the new Filipino society, we must look briefly at the role of each of the important religious efforts in the Islands. Although deprived of its status as the official religion with the advent of U. S. administration in 1898, the Roman Catholic Church remains the principal religious faith of the Republic. The impact of Catholicism reaches far beyond the formalized role of the Church, its clergy and members. Culturally, Catholic concepts condition to a degree even the behavior of Filipinos who do not consider themselves followers of the Church; the limitation upon divorce written into the new Civil Code is only one expression of this. Powerful religious institutions help make the Philippines a "plural" society; these independently supported centers of thought and action guard against a monopoly of authority in government.

Organizationally, the Church in the Archipelago is composed of thirty-two Ecclesiastical Divisions that include 1,448 parishes. Some 3,500 priests are active in the Islands, of whom about one-half are members of religious orders and congregations; more than 80 percent of the latter are foreigners, among whom American, Spanish, Belgian, German and Irish predominate. Sisters number about 4,300 and three out of every four of these are Filipinas. The Church's concern with education is indicated by its management of 119 colleges and universities, 570 high schools and 287 elementary schools. As with all religious organizations in the Republic, it is difficult to determine the exact number of Filipinos who are members of the Catholic Church. The most recent Catholic Directory lists Church membership at slightly more than 20,000,000. But many priests would agree that a substantial proportion of these are nominal Catholics; the shortage of priests available for parish work makes it impossible to serve such a number. With rare exceptions, however, in Christian regions each municipality has its solid core of devout Church members who often also are prominent citizens of the *población*.

Filipinos have observed that in their country Catholicism tends to be the faith of the elements in the society that are socially, financially and politically most dominant, and of the least favored. The history of the Church in the Islands since the first Spanish missionaries arrived by way of Mexico has encouraged this emphasis. Today, however, determined groups within the Church are laboring to alter this role.

While schooling the sons of the elite at Ateneo de Manila and elsewhere, the Jesuits, who have led in giving Filipinos responsibility within their order, are organizing plantation laborers, industrial workers and white collar groups, and devoting themselves to scientific and social research. Through their numerous high schools and colleges, other religious orders of men and women are providing an opportunity for young Filipinos to learn professional skills that afford an avenue for entering the growing middle class. The Salesians of Don Bosco, who came to the Islands a decade ago as refugees from Communism in China, have established several excellent trade schools where young Filipinos master the skills increasingly demanded by an industrializing economy.

The Philippine Independent Church, that numbers among its members roughly one out of every ten Filipinos, now differs substantially from sixty-odd years ago when it was founded largely upon an appeal to nationalism. Known often as the "Aglipayan" Church, after its first bishop, Gregorio Aglipay, it has passed through a period of internal decay and schism to emerge as principally a church of the masses; it does not maintain schools to offer children of its members an opportunity for more consequential careers. The Philippine Independent Church lost much of its initial following when a series of Court decisions ruled that all properties taken over from the Catholics at the beginning of the century must be returned. Attempts of the founders to borrow from Unitarianism —partly because this was the faith of William Howard Taft, who showed a friendly interest in their cause—never were translated into popular understanding within the movement. Prior to World War II the Church neglected systematic training of its clergy and became enmeshed in politics. Following establishment of the Republic, however, new leaders within the Church began to cooperate with the American Episcopal Church. Through this association the Filipino clergy received apostolic succession and more recently the two churches have been moving toward intercommunion. American Episcopalians now are helping train priests for the Philippine Independent Church, which shows promise of assuming a new and more enlightened role in national life.

Numerically the most rapidly expanding religious organization within recent years has been the Iglesia ni Kristo or Church of Christ, which approximates in membership the Philippine Independent Church. It is the creation primarily of one man, Brother Felix Manalo, who founded the Church in 1914, claiming that he had been specially designated as a "messenger from God." Initially, this church, which takes its inspiration from Manalo's interpretation of the Scriptures, was slow to gather converts. But Manalo built an efficient, highly-centralized organization and em-

phasized thorough training of his ministers to deliver sermons in the vernacular tongue and argue flu-
ently in popular discussions on biblical interpretations.
Amidst chaos of war and early postwar years this
strongly authoritarian church won an ever-growing
membership; Filipinos were attracted partly by the
economic and social concern for members' welfare expressed through a cell-like grouping of families. Even
at the height of their power in Central Luzon the
Huk rebels rarely were able to win support in *barrios*
controlled by the Iglesia ni Kristo. With funds effi-
ciently collected from its members the Church builds
impressive chapels complete with upholstered seats,
particularly in Manila, affording them a sense of added
status. The disciplined membership has become a potent "swing group" in elections, usually voting according to the designated preference of Brother Manalo.
Since he has so thoroughly dominated the church to
date, other Filipino religious leaders question whether
the Iglesia ni Kristo can survive a transition in management. It is now winning more educated converts
but it remains primarily a church of farmers and
workers. Despite considerable resources, the Iglesia
ni Kristo has not organized its own schools and so
far it has shown scant interest in the broader social
and economic problems confronting the Republic.

Protestantism, which arrived with the Americans,
has remained numerically limited, gaining about

1,000,000 adherents. Its relative influence, however, is greater than membership suggests. For most of the Filipinos who have been won to this interpretation of Christianity are schoolteachers, lawyers, certified public accountants, mining engineers, and other members of the growing middle class that moulds attitudes among its neighbors. A high percentage of church members are fully active; the Philippine Federation of Christian Churches, that includes most of the traditional Protestant denominations, has some 2,000 full-time Filipino pastors. Early hopes for Protestant harmony and efforts toward united action, which began with a geographic division of missionary effort in the Islands, have not been entirely realized. Emphasis during the period of U. S. administration upon building a public school system inhibited attention to church-supported higher education. Today the Protestants have sixty-six church-related high schools and support two of the better private universities. With some assistance from mission societies abroad they also maintain many excellent hospitals. Like the more independent groups such as the Seventh Day Adventists, they are strong among new settlers on the Mindanao frontier; adoption of a new faith often marks the more adventurous Filipino who breaks with the older pattern of his society.

In addition to the Roman Catholic Church, ninety-six other religious organizations are authorized by the

Philippine Government to solemnize marriage. Many of these are small sects rarely heard from. They include vigorous groups such as the Jehovah's Witnesses, who have rapidly won converts since independence. In many rural communities public concern with religious issues is reminiscent of earlier eras in Europe and North America when great evangelists drew crowds, and preachers of the gospel did not compete with radio and television. Although their interpretations of Christianity may focus upon obscure passages of the Bible and offer little guidance in dealing with broad contemporary issues, these preachers for little known sects are symptoms of religious restlessness. The following they attract is a measure of the challenge confronting established churches in making Christianity more meaningful to Filipinos who are beginning to sense the uncertain tides of a society in transition.

The mosaic of religious belief and practice in the Archipelago is fluid to a degree that often confounds newly arrived missionaries from the West. The *barrio* fiesta that was introduced from Latin America by Spanish priests is today far more than the occasion for honoring the Catholic patron saint of the community. Although they may not attend the special mass held by the Catholic priest on this occasion, non-Catholics flock home for this celebration to visit with relatives and friends and join in the festivities; this is the time when beauty queens may be elected, cockfighting indulged in most vigorously, *zarzuelas* or rural operas be presented, and fortune-tellers, merchants, brass bands and racing enthusiasts all assemble. Despite lack of official sanction by the Church, non-Catholics do occasionally stand up and become godparents of Catholic children. Most Free Masons in the Islands are Catholics, as are the majority of the growing membership in the YMCA's and YWCA's. Country folk who feel their church requires more than they can afford to pay for a baptism or wedding ceremony may go elsewhere for the occasion and yet consider themselves as belonging to their original faith. Particularly among Catholics, it is the women who usually are most devout. Regardless of the Church to which they belong, Filipino Christians tend to accept God as a merciful Father rather than a stern dispenser of eternal justice, a view of their faith that discourages painful inner soul-searching and fortifies an optimistic temperament.

While most pagan minorities cling stubbornly to traditional beliefs, their religious practices have been unable to adjust to the modern world erupting around them. Instead, pagans seeking to join in the larger national life beyond their isolated villages often become Christians. On home visits to their elders they still may join in the ancient ceremonies, viewing them primarily as cultural customs. Old priests who deplore this erosion of their inherited traditions—that often

include a high sense of personal honor and integrity—
may search with despair for novices to school in their
beliefs.

The followers of Islam in the southern Islands
have been encouraged to a new sense of identity by
the emergence of Egypt, Indonesia, Pakistan and
other predominantly Moslem countries as independent states of world consequence. Although the Archipelago holds no major centers of Islamic research and
scholarship and Filipino Moslems must study abroad
to master the learning of their faith, this new bond
promises that the followers of the Prophet will retain their distinct religious identity. While viewing
themselves as Filipinos, they also are increasingly
proud to be Moslems and thus open to the new ideas
astir in Islam.

Filipino expression through the arts reveals a varied and rich cultural heritage from many lands which
now has been digested to a degree where it can begin to evolve a style distinctively its own. For citizens of the Archipelago this is a major achievement.
Unlike their Asian neighbors—the Chinese, the Hin-
dus, the Khmers and the Javanese—they did not profit
in the pre-colonial era from possession of a single
unified state whose rulers were patrons of sculpture,
ceramics, painting and artistic expression in many

146

forms. Nor were there great cities where artisans could work together and exchange the secrets of their crafts. This hindered development of specialized skills and inhibited the accumulation of traditions for such expression. Instead, Filipinos are compelled to sort through a vast jig-saw puzzle of importations from the Orient and the Occident to discover those forms in harmony with their own aspirations.

Architecturally, the Philippines today is the most venturesome land in Asia. The war which destroyed so much also cleared the way for these new ideas in building. When the Spanish first arrived in the Islands, they found the inhabitants living in homes ideally suited to the needs of the setting and the time. The *barangays* or communities were composed of houses constructed largely of the ever-present bamboo, raised on stilts some four to six feet above the ground and roofed with thatch of the *nipa* palm. This cool, clean structure may have been inspired originally from Indonesia. But unlike the long houses of Borneo and the clan residences of some Indonesian peoples, these were chiefly single family homes. A young couple could start life together in a place of their own. Since no all-powerful state levied taxes and supervised public works, they did not erect stone bridges or even permanent piers for vessels docking at the seacoast trading communities. Man-made temples were not an important part of the Filipino scheme of existence. In his temporal and spiritual life the Filipino accommodated himself to nature and lived with it intimately.

Spanish priests who set out to remake the inhabited landscape concentrated first upon building their massive stone churches with designs borrowed from sixteenth-century Europe; many resemble churches erected throughout Mexico and Latin America at the same period. In the Philippines the priests usually marked out the plaza in front with plantings of imported "rain trees" that now have grown massive and gnarled. Around the plaza were grouped official buildings and residences of prominent citizens. These were inspired by Antillian architecture, with a lower story constructed of stone and massive stairways leading to an upper story of wood where the family lived. The principal cities, such as Cebu and Manila, were protected by fortress walls of rock or adobe. To adorn their churches the priests encouraged religious sculpture in wood and stone. And Filipino families and communities developed traditions that continue to this day of carving their fine-grained many-colored hardwoods. Although the great period of religious architecture has passed, postwar reconstruction has seen the rebuilding of the splendid Metropolitan Cathedral of Manila and many lesser structures.

The era of American administration over the Islands provided opportunity for introduction of two distinctive types of public architecture—the school-

148

house, for which the design—with tropical adaptations—was borrowed from the U. S. Middle West, and the massive concrete government structures in Manila patterned upon the "Potomac Greek" of Washington, D. C., and numerous state capitols. This also was a period of road building, when bridging of rivers demanded development of engineering skills. Only within the past three decades has architecture become a major profession; early pioneers brought in Renaissance, Norman, Italian and Spanish forms. As they helped in the massive postwar reconstruction and now share in designing for spreading urbanization, Filipino architects are becoming more versatile in adapting concrete, steel, glass and wood to their needs and climate. From the outside, many a new home in the suburbs appears to have been copied directly from one of the popular American magazines. But interior design and furniture and home furnishings, now a consequential industry, reveal a unique Filipino taste for exquisite line and color. In the new schools, banks, insurance houses and office buildings there is an increasingly happy blend of the traditional and the modern adapted to the Islands.

Filipino contemporary painters are as vigorous as any among their fellow artists in Asia; emergence of these prolific and experimental-minded schools of painters since independence has been facilitated by the very lack of an earlier national tradition. The first Filipino painters to win international recognition were deeply influenced by their late nineteenth century European studies. The two most prominent among these, Juan Luna and Felix Resurrección Hidalgo, continued to favor European subjects over those of their native land. Early in the twentieth century Fernando Amorsolo brought the lively color sense of the early impressionists to portraying Filipino rural folk in their tropical setting with its rich contrasts of brilliant green bamboos, intense sunlight and golden rice harvests. A vigorously experimental school of painting was introduced in 1928 by Victorio C. Edades who soon stimulated a group of like-minded associates in a proliferation of styles.

A new creativity among artists burst upon the Philippine scene following World War II; the years of destruction and privation that erased old patterns also had been a time of genesis. Now in the coffee shops erected along shell-shattered streets they met and talked of a "plastic reality" expressed in colors, shapes, lines and space relationships. Hernando Ocampo led this "neo-realist" group that also included others of talent such as Romeo Tabuena, Fernando Zobel and Arturo Luz. They and their fellow painters won new public understanding and appreciation through creation of the Art Association of the Philippines. When the Philippine Art Gallery was established they found an opportunity for selling their paintings to an ever-widening circle of both wealthy and middle-class collectors. More recently other studios have been established. Sculpture is increasingly appreciated and it is not unlikely that Filipinos working with their rare woods and other materials will approach in creativeness the work of contemporary painters.

Their diverse heritage also has given Filipinos a rare instinct for music and made them among the most natural of dancers. Latin music that first reached the Islands as a part of religious ceremonies introduced by Christian missionaries blended happily with the instinct for rhythm and joy in creating harmony of an earlier era. This pre-Western music still is found among the non-Christian groups. The Moros play the xylophone-like *kolintang* composed of brass gongs similar to the Indonesian *gamelan*. They also are skilled in using native flutes and a two-stringed wooden guitar. Among other ethnic minorities the bamboo jew's-harp, nose flutes, and bamboo guitars are favorites. Introduction of European instruments and more developed musical scales and concepts among a people with these traditions created new opportunities for expression; the guitar, violin and more recently the banjo found a new and congenial home. Young boys in the *barrio* learned to dream of marching down the dusty street playing one of the brassy instruments in the blaring band. Today the "combo," playing Western and indigenous music, has become a favorite; the prevalence of

Filipino dance bands throughout cities of the Far East is one expression of this national talent. Although it has been difficult to replace musicians, instruments, and music lost during the war and more urgent reconstruction was given priority, Manila is again developing its symphony orchestras and smaller instrument ensembles, while the military bands are proving their excellence. Despite the high cost of instruments, Filipino parents are anxious for their daughters to master the piano, and musical skill is a respected talent.

A new delight in things Filipino has encouraged creation of an ever-growing number of dance companies that now make professional tours in Europe and America. Leaders among these are the Bayanihan of Philippine Women's University, the Far Eastern University Dance Troupe and the Barangay of the Philippine Normal College. Inspired by pagan, Islamic, and Christian folk dances, they have developed a varied choreography complete with rich costuming and staging complementing the lithe young dancers. Today there is an energetic search for new native themes that can be translated onto the stage. And European ballet, although it now commands less space on the society page than before the war and has been frowned upon by the Catholic Church, still is considered a desirable social grace for daughters of some of Manila's prominent families. The *rigodon de honor* or stylized minuet by men and women in formal dress remains the favorite for social ceremonies. Filipinos also gladly dance the tango, rumba and more modern steps and new melodies introduced from the West rapidly become popular throughout the Islands.

Although contemporary theater remains underdeveloped as a vehicle for interpreting and expressing issues within the society, two types of folk opera, the *Moro-moro* plays and *zarzuelas,* continue to attract capacity audiences in the rural communities; some large commercial firms maintain troupes of these traveling players as an advertising gesture. Artistic interest in such indigenous creative activity, however, has suffered through the growth of the movie industry. The Philippines offers the third largest foreign market for American films, and stereotypes of Hollywood have left an imprint upon the behavior of younger Filipinos, including boys who delight in cowboy boots and chaps. A domestic movie industry now produces its native versions of American celluloid operas and occasionally movies of broader consequence. It is important in extending use of "movie Tagalog" as a spoken tongue, but the Filipino film industry generally has not attracted talents nor production facilities enabling it to become an artistic arena. Considerable opportunities for employing educational films to advance technology and creative community enterprises have received scant support from the government and private groups.

Literature today most fully reflects both the popular intellectual concern of the mass of ordinary citizens and the essence of the "Filipino soul" as perceived by writers. It had its beginnings in remote prehistory in the great epic poems that were memorized by elders of the community and passed along verbally from one generation to the next; several festive nights are required even now for the priests among the Ifugaos to recite their *Hudhod* and *Alim*. Among the Bicolanos there are elders who still recall portions of their epic, the *Ibalon*. Traces of other epics have been discovered among the peoples of Panay, Ilocos and other Christian regions, and skill at poetic recitation remains an avenue to status among several Moro peoples. Poetic jousts are a popular pastime among rural Filipino Christians in many provinces. Quotations from the Tagalog poetic version of the "Life and Death of Jesus Christ" often form an important part of the wake held for recently deceased family elders. Catholic and Protestant laymen may engage in poetic contests employing their respective versions of the Bible in efforts to prove religious points. In many a *barrio* the *Filosopo* who can banter his neighbors for hours with a play on words is popular; his wit frequently frustrates those who would innovate changes. And Juan Tamad or "Lazy Juan" is a Paul Bunyan type of humorous folk figure who betrays the Filipino delight in discovering ways for making a living without effort, such as lying under a spreading guava tree with his mouth open and waiting for the fruit to drop.

Early Spanish priests reaching the Islands found Filipinos employing an alphabetical system of writing on bark and polished bamboo. While these first missionaries often treated such native records as idolatrous and may have destroyed some written evidence, they also included scholars who have left accounts of their findings. Soon the Spanish introduced printing, first with wood blocks and then type. Early publications, however, were almost entirely religious, including the widely circulated novenas, the *pasión* describing the life of Christ in the vernaculars and catechetical books that also were used in the schools. In time there were published legendary tales, often in verse and inspired by European themes with a local setting. It was this form that the first prominent Filipino Tagalog writer, Francisco Balagtas, chose in the early nineteenth century for his epic romance, *Florante at Laura*. The intellectual renaissance of the late nineteenth century produced a host of versatile writers usually employing Spanish. For the first time Filipinos began critically examining the experience of their people, their heritage and aspirations; essays, poems and novels became part of a propaganda movement for change and independence. José Palma's *Filipinas,* now sung as the national anthem, dates from this period, as do Rizal's great social novels, *Noli Me Tangere* and *El Filibusterismo*. Periodicals such as *La Solidaridad*, founded in Spain, published articles by the expatriates, including Mariano Ponce and Marcelo del Pilar. At home, essayists such as Rafael Palma, Epifanio de los Santos and Antonio Luna stirred a new critical sense among their fellow Filipinos.

Journalism became a consequential pursuit with the arrival of the Americans, and most of today's writers molded their style and themes through the new influence of the popular printed word and mass education. As English gradually replaced Spanish, the short story became more popular than the poem and the essay. With establishment of the Commonwealth, government-sponsored national literary contests awarded prizes for writing in English, Tagalog and Spanish. Filipino writers of this generation who have made a creative contribution to shaping the national conscience are too numerous to mention. Representative of their craft at its best are José Garcia Villa, Manuel E. Arguilla, N. V. M. Gonzales, Nick Joaquin, Carlos Bulosan, R. Zuleta de Costa and Bienvenido N. Santos. They reveal an increasing sureness of literary expression that is one of the marks of their maturing society. However, Philippine publishing and the press have yet to develop a capacity for social scrutiny that would help Filipinos to see themselves and their environment clearly and so to become more deliberate in choice of avenues for national emphasis. War cost the lives of many courageous and talented writers and editors. Postwar confusion compounded by political issues has made some become pamphleteers. But the enormous effort in education now is beginning to generate a hunger for ideas, and there is a ripe opportunity for Filipino writers who would contribute to further integration of their social, religious and artistic heritage.

The cultivation of leisure is an art in the Islands, particularly in the rural regions, and Filipino pastimes reflect this tolerant view of existence. Although books and literary learning are prized, there is such a paucity of reading material in the provinces that the curious youngster finds little to enlarge his horizons. Most private and public libraries were destroyed during the war and since then exchange controls have discouraged private importation of books. Commercial book publishing so far has not become an important domestic industry; a locally printed popular book may sell 1,000 to 2,000 copies. Since no substantial market has been established there is little incentive for writers and publishers to produce in the vernacular languages for readers whose low cash purchasing power and habits discourage creation of book distribution systems. Yet, the popularity of the few lending libraries now in existence testifies to the interest in knowledge of the outer world among Filipinos and the avid determination of many younger people to school themselves.

Filipinos now tend to devote themselves to pastimes that afford group satisfaction. Movies are immensely popular in the cities. In rural areas where electricity is not available the advent of the transistor radio has provided a new focus for community gatherings. In the evening when the farmer has brought his *carabao* in from the field and finished his meal, he and his neighbors may gather at the *barrio* store and listen to news broadcasts and radio programs. The long discussions of politics, crops, prices, and fish that are a traditional part of rural life now have a new point of departure as local citizens speculate upon the implications for them of national and international events. Traditionally, women have worked longer hours than men as housekeeping and child care demanded continuing attention. When leisure was available in rural communities they attended church or gossiped about local affairs. Now the radio also is enlarging their awareness and bringing new ideas into family councils.

Organized recreation differs greatly from one island or ethnic group to the next. Among lowland Christian Filipinos there is hardly a municipality without its cockpit or *gallera*. Officially, cock fights are held only on Saturdays, Sundays, public holidays and at the time of the town *fiesta;* they begin between nine o'clock in the morning and noon and continue almost until sundown. An *aficionado* lavishes great care upon his champion cock, feeding him a special diet, stroking his muscles to keep the bird flexible, and training for the day when the fighter, with a double-bladed spur fixed to his claw, will enter the fray. Betting often is heavy and families have lost their fortunes when a father became overly committed to the merits of a bird he had trained for the bout. After a heated day at the cockpit, a glass or two of *tuba,* made from the fermented sap of the coconut palm, or another local alcoholic beverage quenches the thirst and helps salve feelings that were aroused over the outcome of a match.

Young people are becoming increasingly sports minded. Before the war baseball was immensely popular and Filipinos were among the leading players of the game in the Far East. Now that equipment is difficult to secure they have shifted to playing softball and basketball. Matches between communities are staged regularly and a good player becomes a local hero. In the cities, schools and larger firms have their own basketball teams that play to capacity crowds and are challenged by visiting foreign amateurs and professionals. Boxing commands its devoted band of Filipino followers who support the periodic holding of world championship bouts in the lighter weight classes where Filipinos can compete successfully. Native games include *sipa,* a form of volley ball played with the feet, and *arnis,* or fencing with rattan staffs. When young men and women gather they delight in joking, telling stories, joining in their native dances or singing to the accompaniment of a guitar. More revealing than the pastimes themselves is the spirit with which Filipinos approach leisure; life is fun, they believe, and every effort should be made to keep it so.

# 7.  *Government, Politics and Education*

Among new nations that have emerged within the past two decades few have achieved a stability of government equalling the Philippine Republic. Yet, this is also one of the most open of societies. Filipinos are unusually free to express themselves, as the flamboyant headlines of their newspapers and as their irreverent radio broadcasters reveal. The chief of state may be castigated by orators in Manila's Plaza Miranda with no more serious consequences than a tortuous and much publicized libel suit in the courts. Citizens group themselves in innumerable political action organizations, many of which languish after the first spurt of

enthusiasm. This freedom extends even to a sometimes permissive law enforcement that may lend an
American Wild West touch to provincial politics; the
ambitious must either ally themselves with the local
bosses or challenge them.

Filipino success in making democratic political instruments work for their fragmented Archipelago
traces to more than their Christian heritage first
brought from Spain and their decades of American
tutelage. The Constitution adopted in 1935 provides
for a presidential type of government wherein responsibility is shared with an independent Congress
and Judiciary, and this has lent a permanence to administration not experienced by most new countries
that chose a parliamentary system. Elections are held
every two years under supervision of the independent
Commission on Elections; they serve both as an opportunity for engineering change through the ballot
box and as a social safety valve. Equally vital is an
educational system creating an increasingly literate
electorate with horizons of interest that span the Republic. Key questions for the future concern whether
the political party structure can elevate leaders who
will focus discussion upon real issues affecting the "felt
needs" of *barrio* folk and development of scholarly
research providing sound guides to national action.

The president of the Philippines, holding office in
ornate Malacañang Palace on the Pasig River, is rela-

tively more powerful in domestic affairs than his American counterpart residing in the White House. Constitutionally, the chief executive can suspend elected governors and mayors. He need not share responsibility with the vice-president, who may be elected from another party and has a largely ceremonial role—both are chosen for four-year terms by direct popular vote. And he has inherited the highly centralized administration built up during the era of colonial rule. Through cabinet secretaries whom he appoints the president directs the multifarious activities of the ten regular departments. These are concerned with justice, education, finance, agriculture and natural resources, public works and communications, labor, national defense, health and public welfare, commerce and industry and foreign affairs. Heads of the Office of Economic Coordination, the Social Welfare Administration, and the Department of General Services also sit in on Cabinet meetings as does the presidential press secretary and the executive secretary who manages the office of the president. Another thirty-one special offices are directly responsible to the president, including the Budget Commission, the Bureau of Civil Service, and the National Economic Council. Likewise reporting to the president are the Central Bank, which manages the currency and foreign exchange reserves and supervises private banking, the three government banks and the largely independent

General Auditing Office. Through this labyrinth of government services the president, when vigorous and determined, can insure the influence of his administration on even the most remote islands; as commander-in-chief of the armed forces, he also controls the Philippine Constabulary or national police force. This centralized structure has fostered a sense of national unity despite the geographic, ethnic and familial fragmentation of the Archipelago.

Under American rule authority was first extended to Filipinos through their own elected representatives, and consequently the Congress equals the presidency in traditional influence. A taxation system assuring national government control over most sources of revenue reinforces this. For the twenty-four senators who are elected at large throughout the Islands for six-year terms and Congressmen chosen every four years to represent the 104 districts arbitrate over funds upon which most communities depend for their essential services and public improvements, including schoolhouses, roads, and much else. The "pork barrel bill," as it is popularly known, that Congress enacts annually most obviously betrays this paternalistic political role; each senator and congressman under this provision may allocate from 250,000 to 500,000 *pesos* for public improvements. These frequently are parcelled out with an eye to his political influence as well as for public benefit. In the Filipino scheme of life the members of Congress enjoy rare status, complete with low numbered license plates for their automobiles and the opportunity to extend patronage to their followers and relatives. A barefooted boy growing up in his *barrio* who dreams of reaching the top may have visions of becoming a senator before whom appointed officials give way and all doors open, although the mounting cost of politics and frequent reshuffles in leadership alliances actually make this a hazardous career.

Despite cumbersome legal processes, Filipinos are firmly wedded to the principle of rule by law, and the law offers a favored career for young men and women, including some who may plan to enter government service, politics and business; in a single year successful candidates passing the national bar examinations may number over 2,000. The chief justice and the ten associate justices of the Supreme Court form the apex of this judicial branch of government. Above and apart from politics, they are among the most respected citizens of the Republic and have been firm in ruling upon the constitutionality of legislative and executive acts. The Supreme Court also forms the Presidential Electoral Tribunal, and three justices serve on each of the Senate and House of Representatives Electoral Tribunals together with three members of the majority and second largest party from each House. At lower echelons are the statutory courts that include a Court of Appeals and Courts of First Instance, of which there usually is one in each province—populous provinces may have more and in less settled regions two provinces share a single court. Manila and other chartered cities have their municipal courts and in each of the municipalities there is a Justice of the Peace. Special courts dealing with particular problems include a Court of Agrarian Relations, Court of Industrial Relations, Court of Tax Appeals and Court of Domestic Relations. The Philippines does not employ the jury system. Rather, trial is held before judges who are appointed by the president with approval of the Commission on Appointments composed of members from both houses of Congress. While the Philippine Republic has retained much of Spanish substantive law, it also has adopted Anglo-Saxon procedural law with its greater safeguards for the individual. Decisions appealed from the Philippine Supreme Court to the U. S. Supreme Court during the period of American administration still are cited as precedents.

The Archipelago is divided into fifty-six provinces. Each has its own governor, heading a three-man provincial board, all of whom are elected for four years. Unlike officials of American states, the governor and his staff have only limited administrative authority. The national government holds all residual powers and appoints both the provincial treasurer and the provincial fiscal, who is the chief legal officer. Like-

wise the provincial engineer, the division superintend-
ent of schools, the provincial agriculturists and health
officer serve under their respective departments of the
national government. Although the provincial constabulary detachment reports to the governor, it is to the
Department of National Defense that officers and
men look for logistics and promotion. Since each province has only meager tax revenues of its own and must
depend upon allocations of funds from the national
government, the governor is important chiefly as a
political leader mediating between his citizens and national officials in Manila.

Until recently the 1,284 municipalities were the low-
est level of elected government. Seat of their authority
is the *presidencia* or municipal hall on the plaza of the
*población*. A mayor, vice-mayor and council elected
every four years manage municipal affairs. They are
assisted by a full-time secretary who keeps vital statistics on births, deaths and marriages. Like the province, the municipality has only the most limited of tax
powers and must rely primarily upon allocations from
the national government. Even the municipal Treasurer who collects taxes and manages funds is appointed
from Manila. School teachers, like the municipal agri-
culturist and health personnel, are members of national
government departments. Since the larger landowners,
local businessmen and professionals usually live in the
*población* they tend to dominate municipal govern-

ment; their interests have conditioned its role of informing provincial and national authorities about local conditions and shaped use of public resources for rural progress.

Only within the last five years have the *barrios* that form the base of the pyramid of government in the Islands begun electing their own officials; formerly barrio lieutenants were appointed by the municipal mayor and often represented the concern of those dominant in the *población*. Now residents of the *barrios* choose their own governing councils in a public meeting every two years. This includes a chairman, a vice-chairman for each *sitio* or village in the *barrio* and three councilors—total membership varies from eight to fifteen. Funds available for the council to finance desired improvements still are scant, since by law they are entitled to only 10 percent of the land tax and are empowered to vote only a small surcharge on this. These councils do afford opportunity for the ordinary *tao* or farmer to be heard and provide experience in democratic processes related to problems rural Filipinos know intimately. Throughout some 28,000 *barrios* in the Islands these councils provide an avenue to leadership for citizens who at one time were often ignored.

Most consequential of post-independence moves toward decentralizing government in the Philippines is the increasing election of officials in the thirty-four chartered cities. Beginning with Manila and Quezon City and including such burgeoning towns as Davao and Iligan, these cities hold the most educated, economically advanced, and concerned citizens of the Republic. In managing the urban problems of these largely new cities, a generation of younger Filipinos is mastering the arts of government planning and administration. Chartered cities are acquiring substantial tax revenues of their own, as real estate values mount, and as a result are acquiring greater independence from the national government. It is here that the industrial labor force is beginning to make itself most felt in political action. And these cities are elevating promising new elected leaders to national attention.

Interwoven through and around the governmental structure at every level is the omnipresent influence of politics. Politics may help determine whether a municipal treasurer is assigned to a remote province or permitted to work near Manila, where his children can live at home while going to college. Despite Civil Service regulations, politics can also influence promotion; this also happens in the military. Earlier administrations through the Central Bank, the Monetary Board, Department of Commerce and other agencies, regulated foreign exchange allocations, barter licenses and import permits, and much of overseas trade was affected. Political considerations have also conditioned availability of credit from official lending institutions such as some government banks, the Social Security System and the Government Service Insurance System. As a consequence, Filipinos think of politics not only as a process for selecting officials of the Republic and managing the public purse, but also as a consideration affecting their personal careers and fortunes.

Filipino humorists have defined politics as the country's largest single industry; attention and funds devoted during bi-annual elections lend this partial credence. Politicians both in and out of office find it a way of life. Each who has some stature or promise is surrounded by "followers"—some gain jobs or status by this association, and others reason that identification with their candidate may spare them routine nuisances such as traffic violation tickets. For capturing an election tends to place the winner and his closest associates beyond the law and this fact encourages pre-election terror and violence. Many Filipino private citizens deplore the intrusion of politics into their lives, but cherished popular beliefs contribute to its influence; there is faith that a man can rise from the least privileged of origins, and the simplest farmer may hope his boy will find a place in the sun. The political candidate responds to this belief, implying: "Work for me and make sure your relatives give me their votes. When I am elected your son can come and I will find him a job in Manila." Some politicians subsidize boarding houses in the capital where sons of

170

their provincial followers find free room and board while studying.

Despite the highly personal and fluid character of Filipino politics, the party structure has a permanence rare in Asia. The two parties that garnered the largest totals of votes in the last presidential election—now the Nacionalistas and the Liberals—are authorized by law to name inspectors on the electoral boards in each of more than 40,000 precincts. These electoral boards are legally constituted by the Commission on Elections, which appoints a schoolteacher to serve as chairman and another as poll clerk. They meet on the two days when voters register in September and October, once to revise registration lists and again on election day—the second Tuesday of November—to supervise balloting. For this service each member of the electoral board is paid 25 *pesos* from government funds. Not only does this enable the two major parties to offer their candidates protection against electoral fraud, it also gives them a nationwide organization financed at government expense. Party inspectors are part of machinery that distributes sample ballots and helps voters qualify. In practice, a more demanding literacy requirement usually is met by voters signing their names and writing in those of their candidates. Independent local candidates occasionally win despite this advantage enjoyed by the two major parties, but nationally it has inhibited emergence of successful third party movements.

Control of party machinery is highly centralized. Theoretically, it rests with the national directorates of the parties, composed of incumbent congressmen, senators, governors, and mayors of chartered cities. These directorates rarely meet and actual authority is exercised by twenty-one-man executive committees, headed by the presidents of the parties. It is these executive committees that nominate the inspectors to be named by the Commission on Elections, usually after consultation with local party leaders. The threat to withhold inspectors from a candidate or declare his district a "free zone" where these are divided among several aspirants for office is a feared form of discipline in the hands of the party elders. It is the executive committee of a party that determines whether a congressional candidate is to be nominated by a convention in his district or chosen by them. Likewise, at national conventions of the parties senatorial aspirants have their names placed in nomination. From the forty to sixty so named the executive committees select the eight who will be the party's official candidates during the election held every two years. The majority at party conventions that elect the executive committees is composed of *ex-officio* delegates who are incumbent or former members of Congress, governors, and mayors of chartered cities. Party leadership tends to become self-perpetuating, affording scant opportunity for the unwanted upstart to gain entry. And political chieftains often wield their power very much in the paternal manner, with only remote regard for public opinion.

Within this political structure there is another and more hidden hierarchy of authority—the "pecking order" of wealth needed to finance political action. For in the Philippines, as in the United States and many other lands, winning and holding elective public office have become ever more costly. As the "*peso* price of politics" mounts it tends to restrict opportunities for leadership to the small group who possess the material means or can command the support of affluent backers. The lush expenditures for politics of economic pressure groups representing sugar, tobacco, and new industrial family combines betray the advantages that they expect to gain from political influence. Political attention is therefore often directed from national problems to narrow concern for special interests which wrestle for advantage through the influence of their allies in Congress or the executive. Ahead looms the question of who will speak for the nine out of every ten Filipinos who cannot afford to help finance a politician.

Political leaders themselves are becoming victims of this costly system of campaigning. Today, no one

173

seeking to become a congressman or senator seriously expects to win an election and limit himself to the legal campaign expenditure limit of one year's salary of 7,200 *pesos*. Once in office he knows that his family can hardly live in Manila on this stipend; many spend an equivalent sum only for housing. The purposes for which a candidate requires cash rarely can be fully anticipated, even by a veteran. He must have the usual posters, billboards, stickers, identity cards, and sample ballots, plus newspaper space and radio time if he is running for a city or national office. Then he must support his organization. In the event that he is campaigning for a congressional seat or a governorship, this requires jeeps, gasoline and spending money for each of his leaders in every municipality. Funds are needed to give part-time employment to heads of families with many voters. In a land with chronic unemployment, elections are a time when many rural folk expect to add a bit of cash to their family budgets.

A candidate must entertain, provide cigarettes and soft or hard drinks wherever he goes to hold a rally, and maintain daily open house at his provincial headquarters for some four months before election day. During campaign season many rural Filipinos expect to have quite a few meals free off a candidate, and should his hospitality seem thin the word will spread that he is not as generous as his opponents. Generosity requires slaughtering pigs to be broiled whole over an

174

open fire as *lechón* or butchering goats and cattle for periodic feasts where several hundred may assemble to eat. In the paternal tradition a candidate must have cash ready to hand a few *pesos* to everyone who approaches him with a hard luck story or a genuine need. In key communities he must make financial gestures toward local projects, such as contributing to repair of a typhoon-damaged church. Should the candidate find on election day that his opponents are buying votes, then he must decide whether he should or can match their efforts. It is only the exceptional candidate who expects to make a serious bid for a seat in Congress by spending no more than 50,000 *pesos*. Even unsuccessful contenders have been known to invest as much as 380,000 *pesos*.

Regardless of whether the candidate's own family or his friends advance these sums, most want to recover their investment with a profit. If a candidate has enlisted the backing of a group such as one of Manila's combines of business tycoons they expect him to protect their interests once in Congress. Should the family have advanced the major sum, then they usually anticipate that through influence in Congress they can advance an existing enterprise or be assured of a new opportunity. This may range from a government contract or allocation of reparations equipment to a foreign service appointment for an ambitious son. Rare is the individual who enters Congress a free man

175

to preside over the fate of the Republic with only his conscience as a guide.

Since the concern with personalities and funds is so pervasive in the political arena, regard for issues has been slow to develop—only recently have some of the abler and more idealistically motivated Filipino leaders begun to discuss basic problems with the voters. During the years of American administration almost every candidate campaigned on a platform demanding earlier independence; this was frequently offered as a panacea for all the ills of society. Since independence, the great theme for politicians has been "graft and corruption." The opposition argues that they will clean out the scoundrels and the incumbents insist that they are actually doing better than their predecessors. The Filipino voter has heard so much of this that he is skeptical and rarely becomes incensed. However, recent elections have shown that voters can be aroused when they believe that an official or party is resorting to terror or fraud to retain power. Opportunities for approaching the Filipino voter with ideas that meet his instinctive needs are becoming apparent. The late Magsaysay's political magic was compounded of a promise of social justice as much as personal appeal. Those who would be his heirs are discovering they can make issues such as "*barrio* home rule," decentralization of tax authority, and tenancy reform meaningful to voters. But this requires patient and persistent explanation in countless meetings. They are handicapped by lack of more critical scholarly publications, where ideas are measured against the problems at hand. Collapse of the Huk movement and Communist emphasis upon covert penetration has left the field of social action open. And many an idealistic young Filipino is in search of genuine liberal ideas that could guide progressive political reform in and out of government.

The remarkable progress Filipinos have made during the twentieth century in building a self-governing republic is primarily the result of the extraordinary efforts devoted to education. Particularly is this apparent when the breadth of awareness among citizens in the *barrios* is compared to that of their fellow Asians in rural villages of neighboring countries. For Filipinos the modern world of technology and ideas is not something remote and utterly strange, but a possibility within reach. This creates unique national opportunities and also warns of hazards if they are not fulfilled. In a society where only some 18 percent of the citizens enjoy a per capita annual income above the national average of 378 *pesos* ideas must be fashioned which afford the young Filipino on the move reasonable prospects of realizing his hopes. The very extent of education has become a goad to political and economic performance, but the present quality of schooling does not promise to make this performance possible. The future of this young nation depends substantially upon whether education can command the talents and concern with excellence that are needed for prosperous democratic evolution.

The enormous attention to schooling the young is readily apparent. Education absorbs the largest item, or some 35 percent, of the national budget for current operating expenses; this is almost twice the percentage devoted to national defense. Included is approximately 351,000,000 *pesos* annually for the Department of Education and some 20,000,000 *pesos* for the University of the Philippines and eight other nationally chartered centers of higher learning. Schoolteachers and professors numbering nearly 140,000 comprise the largest contingent of the civil service. The 29,473 public primary, intermediate, secondary, and collegiate institutions they serve bring them into closer contact with citizens throughout the Archipelago than any other group of officials. The scope of private education is also impressive. Twenty-four universities are recognized by the government, including both religious-supported and non-sectarian institutions, plus 315 colleges. There are also 1,751 private kindergarten, primary, intermediate, secondary and vocational schools.

The avid quest of Filipinos for education is revealed in many ways. A surprising proportion of *barrio* schoolhouses have been constructed through contributions of citizens organized by the P.T.A.'s and other groups. There are few benefits a candidate seeking public office can promise a community that rate higher than an addition to their schoolhouse. The simplest *tao* sees education for his children as the most treasured heritage he can leave them; a family will sacrifice almost every other advantage in favor of schooling for at least one of its sons, who in turn is expected to help the others. Although Filipinos like Americans tend to equate education with earning potential, a degree in itself confers status. A young man who returns to his provincial home after passing the national bar examinations feels assured of respectful listeners and a prominent role in community deliberations, regardless of whether or not he actually practices law. As a consequence, the schoolteacher commands a respect in rural communities comparable to that of his or her counterpart in the American Middle West half a century ago. The teacher's advice is sought on innumerable personal problems and the schoolhouse is the focus for much of *barrio* life.

Filipinos generally accept those goals for education defined by idealistic Americans founding the system in the Islands; they were ably stated by Joseph Ralston Hayden, who shared in this enterprise as the last vice-governor:

"The most important of these goals have been: to

179

wipe out illiteracy; to make English the common second language of all the people; to give every Filipino child at least a modern elementary education designed to develop him as a patriotic citizen and as a politically, socially, and economically competent member of society; through a limited number of secondary schools and institutions of higher learning, to develop a body of trained and cultured citizens from which leadership at its various levels may be expected to emerge. A more recently adopted objective is to make modified Tagalog a common Philippine language."

Of late these objectives have been altered to include use of the vernacular tongue of the community as the language of instruction during the first two years of primary schooling, while English and Pilipino—the national language—are taught as second languages, with a later shift to instruction in English. Also, Spanish has been added as a required subject at the collegiate level, to the distress of many students who find the "language load" overly demanding. The issue of religious instruction in public schools during class hours by private teachers has caused some controversy. But the national commitment to insure an educated citizenry as called for in the constitution remains among the foremost of the avowed purposes of government.

Actual schooling provided for many Filipinos, however, falls critically short of these objectives. More

than 30 percent of school-age children at present re-
receive no formal education; either schools and teachers are not available or their parents feel themselves
unable to afford the cost of books, supplies, better
clothing, and the like needed by students. Almost every
year the Congress adds to the appropriation for opening additional schools or extension classes. Still the lag
created by the war and burgeoning population exceeds
available resources. Among the children who do enroll
in the public primary schools only about 50 percent
complete the first four years. This has meant that
many a child who did attend school acquired at best
a smattering of familiarity with subjects taught. Only
some 30 per cent of the students who start school
complete the fifth and sixth grades—the seventh and
eighth grades are not taught in public schools—and
enter high school, and a substantially smaller proportion of these graduate.

For the more than 5,000,000 young Filipinos now
receiving their education, of whom the vast majority
are in the public elementary schools, the quality of
the learning process is often tragically inadequate. The
most graphic symptom of this is the shortage of textbooks and other reading materials. Most of these were
destroyed by the war and only a fraction have been
replaced. In the better public elementary schools it
is common to find three to ten students sharing
one battered textbook, and some of these are rented.

There are *barrio* schools that until recently lacked even one textbook for an entire class. As a consequence, teachers are compelled to improvise, writing out lessons on a blackboard or seeking the assistance of older students to copy all study assignments that then can be passed around to others. Inevitably, this places an emphasis upon memorization rather than study and affords the young Filipino with curiosity little upon which to nurture his intellect. Both the Philippine Government and the U. S. Government, through its war damage payments and economic aid, have been slow to act on this problem. Commercial publishing interests anxious to protect their market are permitted to take precedence over the needs of the younger generation.

A drastic decline in the quality of English used by teachers and students is crippling the school system. Although theirs is among the half a dozen most populous nations relying upon English as a language of education and government, Filipinos long have favored their own usage, including some florid phrases. Formerly those employing the language usually mastered it. Facility in speaking suffered, however, after establishment of the Commonwealth. Congress then forbade enforcement of an earlier rule that children in school also use English during play hours—some elected representatives had themselves been penalized when young for infraction of this rule. Wartime interruption in teacher training made those who staffed the schools after independence less qualified, while students also had missed four or five years of instruction.

Partially in response to this dilemma, the Department of Education determined upon use of the vernacular languages for instruction during the first two years before shifting to English; the aim is to insure that students who do not go beyond primary school are enabled to read and write in the languages of their homes. This promises no adequate solution for the more ambitious student, who often remains severely handicapped. Veteran Filipino educators estimate that one-half of the students seeking college admission lack the mastery of English necessary to comprehend their assigned texts. Denied confident knowledge of the language through which they are learning, their entire educational experience is inhibited. This discourages verbal exactness and curtails critical thought.

Deterioration in the quality of public schools is encouraging an ever greater number of Filipino parents to send their children to better private and chiefly parochial elementary schools. Only a small minority of families can afford the tuition, although mastery of fluent English is a prized mark of status for their sons and daughters. As a consequence the Philippines is developing a two-class society; an elite is graduated from private schools and the better public schools, usually located in or near cities, and their command of English gives them access to the professions, the new skills of technology, and management and government posts. The other class is composed of the majority of rural children, whose schooling is so sketchy that in actual practice even the road to self-education is blocked. This tends to make a mirage of the hopes of many farm families that through schooling their children may be enabled to enjoy a brighter future.

These disastrous trends are reflected at the collegiate level. The University of the Philippines and the best private institutions including Ateneo de Manila University, Silliman University in Dumaguete, Philippine Women's University and a few others maintain reputable standards for admission. Thus they insure a student body able to profit from the best that professors have to offer. But the demand for an education, or at least a degree, far exceeds the enrollment these institutions can accept and the capacity of most students to qualify. This encourages a new and often cynical practice of "education for a profit." Both private stock corporations and some religious groups have organized colleges and universities that are managed so as to make money. Stocks of some among these dividend-paying institutions are sold on the exchange. Inevitably, profits are made at the expense of quality. Among the quarter of a million college students in the Philippines are many whose diplomas will testify at best to a haphazard schooling, emphasizing memorization and the formality of passing examinations. Vested interests so far have frustrated most efforts of conscientious private scholars and public officials to impose standards. Popular Filipino clamor for schooling regardless of content discourages all but the rare leader from making this a public issue.

Such is the crucible that is producing for the Republic a few well-trained leaders and a large "intellectual proletariat." It is reflected throughout the society. Only after surmounting formidable hurdles has the new National Science Development Board now been able to initiate the research that is so vital to effective use of resources and people in emerging new lands. In many fields there is a chronic shortage of men and women who possess both the training and instinct for critically appraising their environment. The Philippine Medical Association estimates that some 15,000 physicians are registered in the Islands, of whom some 65 percent are in active practice; the ratio of doctors to patients is among the highest in Asia. Among them are doctors of great skill and dedication and they have led in encouraging an understanding of the need for quality within the medical profession and other scientific fields. Many also are graduates of medical schools managed for profit and these are prominent among the one-third of all candidates who have failed to pass certification examinations that would enable them to seek more advanced training

185

in American hospitals. Similar problems of imposing standards beset other professions. While the tantalizing frontier of chemurgy has excited the interest of a small band of pioneers they have difficulty finding able technicians. The world of tropical medicinal plants has been little explored, although a few botanists have pointed the way to promising possibilities. Yet, the fragmented Archipelago is a ready-made laboratory, not only because of its wealth of flora and fauna but also through the opportunities it offers for "learning from life" with disciplines such as geographic pathology; the numerous ethnic minorities have accumulated experience widely at variance with the now more standardized existence of the West.

Institutional philanthropy has been slow to develop in the Archipelago. Much will depend upon how vigorously this tradition which has been so vital to healthy societies elsewhere is adopted by Filipinos. Only creation of a public and private educational system that does afford greater creative opportunity to the young with talent can guard against making a mockery of the democratic promises of the Republic. In an era of contending ideologies, freedom can be defended only if inherited traditions and today's aspirations are blended to bring about needed change without sacrifice of the individual. Filipinos, with an instinct for such democratic ways, need centers for research that afford national "self insight," from which ideas can emerge to challenge the young and provide their leaders with guides to the increasingly complex problems they must manage.

The Republic is fortunate in possessing possibly the most free and vigorous press and mass communications media in Southeast Asia. Their influence is pervasive, even in the provinces. Six large English language daily newspapers are published in Manila; they range in circulation from 16,000 to about 120,000. The daily press also includes two newspapers in Tagalog, one in Spanish and five publications in Chinese. National weeklies are among the most consequential molders of public opinion. The five largest in English have circulations that vary from 40,000 to 155,000 and are matched in distribution by the most popular of the vernacular weeklies. A dozen educational magazines are printed each month, as well as twenty-two trade journals and numerous specialized publications for doctors, lawyers, labor unions, women, tourists, veterans, sports enthusiasts and religious groups. Comics and movie magazines, chiefly in the vernacular, have an impressive circulation. The major provincial cities are served by their own local newspapers that usually have 3,000 to 8,000 circulation and appear weekly in English.

Within recent years radio broadcasting has become a major industry and today some 160 stations are on the air. Most powerful commercial stations are part of the eight leading networks. Radio broadcasting also is an important concern of religious groups, some universities, and the government. In the provinces small stations are becoming local "newspapers of the air" since this medium adapts itself easily to the numerous dialects employed by Filipinos in the home. And commentators are among the better known personalities emerging to command public attention and sometimes a devoted following. The particular adaptability of radio to this Archipelago is reflected in the use throughout the Islands of 1,500,000 radio receivers, including transistors. Seven television stations now are operating. The estimated 150,000 television receiving sets are concentrated in the few large cities served by dependable electric power throughout twenty-four hours of the day. As and when transistor television receivers become available this may become a consequential medium for informing barrio folk and fostering a greater feeling of national unity.

Existence of such a varied and extensive press and communications industry means that Filipinos throughout the land increasingly are becoming aware of all that the twentieth century has produced through the proliferation of man's genius. It insures that events which stir the national capital have their repercussions in the remote *barrios*. To date most important radio and television stations are controlled by relatively few firms, for the Republic has not safeguarded itself with curbs against a concentration in ownership of these media. But the greatest challenge remains one of improving the quality of reporting, comment, and programming. Filipinos have proven extraordinarily skillful at dissecting their own political behavior. They have yet to demonstrate a similar capacity for examining the social, economic, and human problems confronting the Republic. The press and mass media have a major opportunity to elevate and sharpen the focus of the "universe of public discourse." Their success in doing so will go far toward determining the sort of life Filipinos will live during the decades ahead when they are molding institutions and attitudes in these the national formative years.

## 8.   The Philippines and the Future

It is rare to find a new nation with an opportunity
for initiative in international relations such as is available to the Philippine Republic. In Asia, yet not entirely of it, the Archipelago so long has been a cross-
roads of influences that Filipinos are at home both in
the East and the West. The Islands are so situated as
to be physically somewhat detached from the critical
events shaking the adjacent mainland. The waters of
the South China Sea and the U. S. defensive shield that
guards their homeland give Filipinos a latitude in their
choice of action abroad not available to other smaller
countries that must co-exist on the border of one of
the great continental powers. Likewise, the wealth of

190

land and natural resources and their relatively more developed economy make the Republic less dependent upon foreign assistance. Filipinos are so preoccupied with their own internal political and commercial pursuits, however, that they give relatively little attention to developments elsewhere, even in neighboring Southeast Asia. Still to be created are facilities for encouraging a more informed public opinion on foreign issues. The Republic also needs a larger corps of able professional diplomats to inform its leaders and chart a truly independent and constructive course abroad. Only as they take a perceptive and sympathetic interest in the affairs of other Asian nations can Filipinos expect to transmit an appreciation of their democratic heritage.

Most framers of the Constitution originally assumed that they could quickly and safely move toward complete self-reliance; in the mid-1930's before the outbreak of the Sino-Japanese War external threats seemed remote. The traumatic experience of Japanese occupation shocked Filipinos and convinced most that they alone could not guarantee future security for their Archipelago. The result was negotiation of an agreement in 1947 whereby the United States was awarded military bases in return for assuming the major burden of external defense. The largest of these are the Clark Air Force-Fort Stotsenburg Reservation in Central Luzon, the Subic Bay Naval Base and adjacent

Cubi Point Naval Air Station on Southwestern Luzon and the Sangley Point Naval Base at Cavite on the Bay opposite Manila. They are now held by the United States under long-term lease and most of the thorny problems of use and jurisdiction have been resolved to mutual satisfaction. It is from these establishments that the U. S. Thirteenth Air Force, the U. S. Seventh Fleet and numerous supporting services operate to defend the vast region from the Bay of Bengal to the Formosa Straits. This defensive arrangement now permits the Philippines to limit its military establishment to some 45,000 officers and men and spares the Republic the financial burden and political hazards of maintaining a large army.

The evolution of economic independence has been more rapid. During the decades of U. S. administration the Philippine economy had become substantially dependent upon duty-free access of its products to the American market and its share of the high-priced sugar quota. Many firms in the Islands also relied upon the advantageous entry of U. S. products including equipment and automobiles, for which distribution systems had been established. The original provisions for separating the two economies were modified by the Laurel-Langley Agreement signed in 1955. This accelerated the rate at which the Philippines can fix a graduated tariff upon imported American products, while exports to the U. S. will be liable for slower imposition of regular duties. The termination date for this agreement is 1974. Until then Americans are assured of equal opportunities with citizens of the Republic, to the extent that these are reciprocated by respective state and federal laws in the U. S. Although the "parity" provision in the "Bell Act" of the U. S. Congress that regulated economic arrangements for independence was criticized at the time, subsequent "nationalization" moves by the Philippine Congress have demonstrated its validity; many who made their homes in the Islands, including Filipinos retired from the U. S. Armed Services, were American citizens and would otherwise have been unjustly penalized. The original provision linking the value of the *peso* to that of the dollar no longer is binding and Filipinos now have full management over their own currency. As evidence of this, President Macapagal on January 22, 1962 ordered the control of the *peso* lifted and declared that the exchange rate was henceforth to be free. Likewise, emergence of a self-confident and powerful indigenous business class with control over most banks and other major sources of credit promises to make the issue of "alien" commercial activities largely a problem of the past. There still are some who would violate the Constitution by denying equality to naturalized citizens; often they represent special interests seeking a scapegoat. But the great majority of Fili-

pinos endorse the principle of equality before the law
that they see as the guardian of their individual rights.

The security of the Republic relates directly to this
question of citizenship. Unless the 500,000 Chinese
living in the Islands are absorbed as confident and constructive members of the community their need for a
powerful outside protector could make them a fifth
column for a Red China determined to wield ever
greater influence throughout East and South Asia.
Although the Communists have their ideological dis-
ciples among some Filipino intellectuals who are seeking to capitalize upon nationalism and cement an alliance with several moneyed groups, their failure to
deal forthrightly with social issues denies them a popular following. Since the abortive Huk revolt the Communist Party also has been outlawed and many of its
leaders imprisoned. These twin developments inhibit
Peking's prospects for finding recruits for its revolutionary crusade among Filipinos while they retain faith
in the elective political process. Responsible leaders of
the Republic are fearful of the consequences if they
open trade with Communist China and the Chinese
minority in the Islands becomes linked through commerce with the mainland. This consideration, combined
with fear of totalitarian methods and concern for their
defenses, has led successive presidents to reject all
suggestions for establishing diplomatic relations with
Peking. Simultaneously the Philippines has maintained

formal and friendly ties with the Chinese Nationalist Government on Formosa.

In international councils the Philippines regularly has stood as a dependable ally with the United States despite criticism from some more neutralist-oriented Asian neighbors. This posture of the Republic traces to more than long-term ties with America and dependence upon U. S. defense efforts. It reflects a genuine sharing of mutual concern for freedom and a way of life deeply influenced by Christianity. Filipinos have been more impatient than Americans to see the Southeast Asia Treaty Organization, created in Manila in 1954, either given real substance or replaced with a more viable instrument. Their concern is expressed not only at the conference table but also on the scene. Today Filipino technicians, doctors, nurses and private firms are prominent in assisting development in Laos, South Vietnam and other neighboring lands. These Filipinos build personal friendships and return home with a knowledge of the languages, religions, and problems of their neighbors that expands the awareness of Asia in their families and communities.

Viewing the future, responsible Filipino leaders are reasonably sanguine about their Republic's capacity to engineer internally the progress needed to give greater substance to their democratic aspirations. The achievements of the past six decades confirm this promise.

For in a remarkably brief span of time Filipinos have transformed their society so that it now can digest new ideas and technology. They have learned to manage this so that these innovations do largely conform to popular "felt needs," thus insuring increasing integration of their patrimony. There is a growing conviction, however, that old patterns of national preoccupation will prove inadequate for insuring a viable and peaceful evolution. The time is past when any country can remain "a group of islands unto themselves." Particularly is this so for the Philippines which has as neighbors several of the world's most populous, burgeoning states, states that are now experiencing revolutionary changes guided by alien ideologies. Inevitably, a small new Republic that sees itself so surrounded fears it may be engulfed and denied the opportunity to continue its own traditions of growth.

Neither thoughtful Filipinos nor their American counterparts, with whom they have been associated so closely in this century, have so far discovered a definite alternative to present arrangements. There is an increasing awareness, however, that the countries on the rim of the world's largest ocean may have no alternative for survival but to assemble in a community of the Pacific. For nearly four centuries the lands on both the eastern and western shores of these waters have shared many formative experiences. Development of modern communications and transportation is shrinking the distances that once held them apart. The broad waters of the Pacific are becoming highways for moving the trade of these increasingly interdependent economies. Appreciation of their common interests is growing among some of the Latin American peoples, who were also deeply influenced by Spanish Christian colonization, Australians and New Zealanders, whose cultural heritage traces to Great Britain, and the Japanese, whose lives have been so intimately affected by America. There are Filipinos who feel that their national experience in accepting religion, science, and democratic political forms brought from the West and fitting these to their own needs has been sufficiently creative to merit their Republic a major role in such an international enterprise.

# Bibliography

ACHUTEGUI, S.J., PEDRO S. DE and MIGUEL A. BERNAD, S.J. *Religious Revolution in the Philippines.* Manila: Ateneo de Manila, 1960.

BROWN, WILLIAM H. *Useful Plants of the Philippines.* Volumes I, II & III. Manila: Bureau of Printing, 1951.

BULOSAN, CARLOS. *The Laughter of My Father.* New York: Harcourt Brace [1944].

COLE, FAY-COOPER. *The Peoples of Malaysia.* New York: D. Van Nostrand Company, Inc., 1945.

COSTA, S.J., H. DE LA. *The Trial of Rizal.* Manila: Ateneo de Manila University Press, 1961.

EGGAN, FRED, EVETT D. HESTER, NORTON S. GINSBURG, and staff. *Area Handbook on the Philippines.* 4 volumes. New Haven: Human Relations Area Files, Inc., 1956.

FORBES, W. CAMERON. *The Philippine Islands.* Cambridge: Harvard University Press, 1945. (Condensed from 1928 two-volume edition.)

GALANG, F. G. *Fruit and Nut Growing in the Philippines.* Malabon, Rizal: The Araneta Institute of Agriculture Press, 1955.

HARTENDROP, A. V. H. *History of Industry and Trade of the Philippines.* Manila: American Chamber of Commerce of the Philippines, Inc., 1958.

HAYDEN, J. RALSTON. *The Philippines: A Study in National Development.* New York: Macmillan, 1947.

JENKINS, SHIRLEY. *American Economic Policy Toward the Philippines.* Stanford, California: Stanford University Press, 1954.

MANUEL, E. ARSENIO. *Dictionary of Philippine Biography.* Quezon City: Filipiniana Publications, 1955.

MORTON, LOUIS. *The Fall of the Philippines* in the U. S. Army in World War II series. Washington, D. C.: Office of the Chief of Military History, Department of the Army, 1953.

PALMA, RAFAEL. *The Pride of the Malay Race.* Translated from Spanish by Ramon Ozaeta. New York: Prentice-Hall, 1949.

PECSON, GERONIMA T. and MARIA RACELIS. *Tales of the American Teachers in the Philippines.* Manila: Carmelo & Bauermann, Inc., 1959.

PHELAN, JOHN LEDDY. *The Hispanization of the Philippines.* Madison, Wisconsin: University of Wisconsin Press, 1959.

QUIRINO, CARLOS. *Magsaysay of the Philippines.* Quezon City: Phoenix Press, Inc., 1958.

QUIRINO, ELISEO and VICENTE M. HILARIO. *Thinking for Ourselves.* Manila: Oriental Commercial Company, 1924.

QUISUMBING, EDUARDO. *Medicinal Plants of the Philippines.* Manila: Bureau of Printing, 1951.

RAVENHOLT, ALBERT. American Universities Field Staff reports series published from 1951 to 1961 at 366 Madison Avenue, New York 17, N. Y.

RAVENHOLT, ALBERT. The Philippine Republic; A Decade of Independence. Chicago, Lead Article in Britannica Book of the Year 1957 by Encyclopaedia Britannica, Inc.

RIZAL, JOSE. *Noli Me Tangere,* published in English as *The Social Cancer.* Translated by Charles E. Derbyshire. Manila: Philippine Education Co., 1912.

RIZAL, JOSE. *The Lost Eden.* Translated by Leon Ma. Guerrero from the Spanish *Noli Me Tangere.* Bloomington: Indiana University Press, 1961.

RIZAL, JOSE. *El Filibusterismo,* a sequel to *Noli Me Tangere,* published in English as *The Reign of Greed.* Translated by Charles E. Derbyshire. Manila: Philippine Education Co., 1912.

RIZAL, JOSE. *The Subversive.* Translated by Leon Ma. Guerrero from the Spanish *El Filibusterismo.* Bloomington: Indiana University Press, in preparation.

ROBEQUAIN, CHARLES. *Malaya, Indonesia, Borneo and the Philippines.* Translated by E. D. Laborde. London: Longmans, Green and Co. Ltd., 1958.

SCHURZ, WILLIAM LYTLE. *The Manila Galleon.* New York: E. P. Dutton & Co., Inc. (In Paperback edition.)

TAYAG, RENATO D. *The Sinners of Angeles.* Privately Published by the Author; Manila, 1960.

TAYLOR, CARL N. *Odessey of the Islands.* New York: Charles Scribner's Sons, 1936.

VILLALUZ, DOMICIANO K. *Fish Farming in the Philippines.* Manila: Bookman, Inc., 1953.

WURFEL, DAVID. Philippine Section of *Governments and Politics of Southeast Asia.* Ithaca, New York: Cornell University Press, 1959.

YOUNGHUSBAND, MAJOR G. J. *The Philippines and Round About.* London: Macmillan and Co., Limited, 1899.

# Index

Abaca, 103
Aborigines, 13–26, 28–36, 58
Agriculture, 41–42, 96–112; *see
    also,* name of specific crop
Aguinaldo, Emilio, 49, 53, 54
American occupation, *see*
    United States
Animals, 9–12, 28–29, 112
Anthropology, *see* Aborigines
Architecture, 147–149
Area, 3
Armed forces, 81–83
    U. S. bases, 191–192
Arts, 146–157
Assembly, *see* Legislature

Bananas, 110
*Barangays,* 32, 42
Bonifacio, Andres, 49
Botany, *see* Plants

Catholic church, 38–41, 136–140
    decline of influence, 46–47
    during U. S. occupation, 60
    organization of, 138–139
    town planning by, 41, 148

Children, 127–128
Chinese, 25–26, 44–46, 187,
    194–195
Chinese occupation, 34–35
Church of Christ, *see* Iglesia ni
    Kristo

Cities, 20–26, 168–169; *see also*
    Municipal government,
    name of specific city
Citizenship, 193–194
Climate, 2–3, 7–8
Cock fighting, 158–159
Cocoanuts, 97–100
Colleges and universities, 178,
    184–185
Colonial periods, 27–70
Communism, 78–81, 194; *see
    also Hukbalahap*
Congress, *see* Legislature
Cooperatives, 131
Copper, 118–119
Corn, 108–109
Corruption, 76–77, 80–81, 130–
    132, 175–176
Courts, 165–166

Dance, 152–153
Dewey, George, 52
Diet, *see* Food

Earthquakes, 6
Economic conditions, 72–73, 75–
    76, 83–84, 95–125, 192–193
Education, 47, 58–60, 177–185
    cost of, 178
    shortage of textbooks, 181–
    182
Elections, 64, 80, 85, 87–88,
    91–93, 171–177